Ettore Sottsass

Ettore Sottsass and the Poetry of Things

Deyan Sudjic

Intro-
duction

7

Ettore Sottsass was a man who set out to leave as many clues as he could for his future biographers. His parents kept every letter that he sent to them during World War II. He got them back when he came home, and filed them away in neatly stacked bundles, like bricks of banknotes, held together by fraying rubber bands that have now grown brittle with age. Sottsass kept every negative of every photograph that he took during that war. He kept his passports and his military identity papers — still creased and folded from the years that he carried them in his grey-green officer's tunic. He also kept every book in his father's architectural library. And he kept his father's high-school diploma, which is written in German reflecting the fact that Sottsass senior was born in Sud Tirol, the German name for the Trentino and had Austro-Hungarian citizenship as one of the Empire's Italian-speaking minority.

From the volume of what survives, it seems that he kept almost every drawing that he ever did — from his childhood scribbles of a town square made in 1924, to the sketchbook that he used almost until the day he died in 2007. Sottsass was a brilliant draughtsman, he could draw perfect circles unaided with either hand, and he drew constantly. He lived through a time when paper was precious and used whatever scraps he could find. What appears on the back of the drawing is sometimes as revealing of what he was doing and where he was, as the material on the face side. He drew on the reverse of printers' calendars, on the back of posters and on old layout sheets from *Industrial Design* magazine that he salvaged whilst in New York working for the designer George Nelson. He made notes on stationery that had originally been designed for a doctor in Turin.

A few drawings were given away as gifts to friends but this did little to shrink the size of his collection. He donated a substantial number of drawings and a selection of gouache sketches, made when he was designing typewriters and adding machines for Olivetti, to the Centre Pompidou in Paris. The Centre holds other drawings from every stage of his career as well as physical examples of his work. What is not in Paris is kept in the University of Parma's archive, housed in a sixteenth-century former monastery in the meadows outside the city. Clearing his filing cabinets in 1979, just before he established Sottsass Associati, he donated 14,000 drawings, sketches, notes and paintings to the university. It's the place to find the letter that Sottsass wrote to himself in 1957 when he was commissioned by Adriano Olivetti to shape the company's first mainframe computer, the Elea 9003. 'What should a computer look like?' he asked. 'Not like a washing machine.'

Sottsass looked after his father's archive until he placed it in the Museo di Arte Moderna e Contemporanea di Trento e Rovereto. Many of his own remarkable photographs — portraits of Ernest Hemingway, Alice B. Toklas and Picasso, Ezra Pound and Allen Ginsberg among them — were donated to the Fondazione Benetton Studi Ricerche in Treviso to complement the papers of his first wife, Fernanda Pivano. Barbara Radice, Sottsass's companion for the last thirty years of his life, maintains an apartment on the Via Pontaccio in Milan as a third archive for his personal papers. The pen-and-ink sketch of Ashoka, the table lamp that he produced for the first Memphis collection in 1981 with its multiple light fittings, each attached to the end of an undulating laminate-faced arm, suggesting a basketful of snakes as drawn by a Cubist, is in one of his notebooks there. So too, are the collected issues of *Terrazzo*, the magazine that he and Radice produced together.

Sottsass took photographs all the time. He left behind thousands of pictures made with the succession of analogue cameras that he owned during the course of his life. In the digital world, where every smartphone can be used to upload a constant stream of images to various social media platforms, such prolific use of a camera is not unusual. In the days of film, negatives and photographic prints it was time consuming, costly and exceptional. Sottsass photographed everything. The hotels he stayed in, the airports he passed through, the temples he saw in Thailand, the deserts he experienced in Egypt. Throughout their years together, Sottsass and Radice shared a camera and recorded the places they went, the people they met and the intimate details of their lives together. Radice photographed Sottsass sleeping in the departure lounge of Tahiti's tiny airport and pictured him wearing a stetson in the mountains of Colorado. Sottsass recorded her in the snow on the terrace of their apartment in Milan and on a water taxi on the Grand Canal in Venice. In the delirious year that they met, they recorded themselves everywhere — setting up the camera on a time delay, before posing in each other's arms. After Sottsass's death, Radice carefully sifted through the countless images that they had taken together, printed them on coated paper and filed them away in a set of linen-covered boxes.

The words that Sottsass left behind, as much as the images he made, are an important part of understanding the meaning of his particular contribution to design. A collection of his writings, *Scritti,* came out during his lifetime. After his death, Radice published the fragmentary autobiography *Scritto di Notte* that he worked on for some years. Sottsass wrote continuously throughout his long life — often in his unmistakable block-capital handwriting. He had an unusual gift as a storyteller and he could write as deftly as he could draw. His stories shaped the objects that he designed; they reflected his life, and the use that he made of his personal experiences in his work. He would write about his travels, as well as recording them in his drawings and his photographs. Talking about the two weeks that he and Pivano spent with Ernest Hemingway in Cuba, Sottsass described how the writer would begin each morning with a drink, and start telling him a story. 'It was always the same story, but told a little differently.' Sottsass was more sober, but told his stories that way too.

He made his life into the raw material for what, at times, could sound like an epic narrative of alienation and deprivation (one that never quite matched the facts of his relatively privileged existence). He was never wealthy despite his fame and he talked about experiencing grinding poverty and hunger. He talked about being an outsider and about his sense of isolation. He wrote about desperate days in damp and freezing basement rooms. Undoubtedly there were some, but he was the son of an architect successful enough to build his own house in Turin. And Pivano, his first wife, came from a wealthy banking family.

Through Pivano, Sottsass met Picasso and Alice B. Toklas, Jack Kerouac, Allen Ginsberg, Gregory Corso, Constantin Brancusi and Andy Warhol. They met or socialized with almost every key figure in the cultural life of Europe in the mid-twentieth-century. Karl Lagerfeld filled his apartment in Monte Carlo with Sottsass's furniture. Sottsass decorated a boat for billionaire art collector Jean Pigozzi, and built a black slate house for the influential art dealer Bruno Bischofberger. His second wife, Barbara Radice, is a writer and a critic, the daughter of Mario Radice, one of the most distinguished Italian artists of the twentieth century. Sottsass and Radice holidayed with Helmut Newton, and with the American billionaire Max Palevsky.

Perhaps the most telling clue as to what, and who, really mattered to him in his long life is a boxed-set of lithographs created when he was eighty-two to mark the turn of the millennium. The most discomforting and the most revealing of them is an image that shows thirty deftly delineated faces, each of them placed on a little ochre-coloured plinth. At first sight they could be taken as light-hearted caricatures but closer inspection reveals that they are death masks. The eyes are closed and every face has been lightly scribbled over — cancelled out — to show that they represent a life now expired. Those pictured were Sottsass's friends, mentors and heroes. The portraits include his parents —his father had died almost half a century earlier, aged just sixty-one, to the continuing distress of his son. There are images of Rosetta and Mario Radice, Barbara's parents. Radice, like Sottsass, had been an officer in the Alpini —Italy's elite mountain troops — in two wars. Radice and Sottsass had learned the same songs; Radice taught them to his daughter and she sang them with Sottsass as he had once done with his army comrades. Radice, born in Como, had been a childhood friend of the architect Giuseppe Terragni — his two most considerable works did not survive the war: the huge abstract sculpture he designed for the grounds of the Milan Triennale was smashed by a British bomb and all eight murals that he made for Terragni's Fascist Headquarters in Como were destroyed in a misplaced burst of post-war de-fascistization, simply because one of them included a portrait of Mussolini. In the process, one of the great acts of collaboration between art and architecture was lost.

Another of the faces in the lithographic sequence belongs to the woman who cleaned Sottsass's holiday home on the island of Filicudi. And there is also Corporal Mario Trezza; a member of the platoon that Lieutenant Sottsass commanded in World War II. Trezza was killed in Montenegro by German machine guns in the wake of Italy's catastrophically inept surrender in 1943. Also appearing is Roberto Olivetti, the man whose father had the extraordinary idea of asking Sottsass, who had previously done little more than design low-cost housing and manufacture fruit bowls, to work on the Elea 9003. More than simply an employer, Olivetti once paid for a dangerously ill Sottsass to travel to California to visit the only doctor who could save his life. There is also a drawing of George Nelson, the American industrial designer. Sottsass worked for him only briefly, but the experience changed his view of the world. One head, simply named Allen, is in memory of Allen Ginsberg. There are other designers and architects whom Sottsass knew and respected, such as Carlo Mollino, Carlo Scarpa, Shiro Kuramata and Aldo Rossi. Like Sottsass, these were all people somewhat out of the architectural mainstream but with a distinctive, highly personal approach. There is an image of Mario Tchou, the brilliant engineer responsible for Olivetti's Elea programme, and another face belongs to Luigi Spazzapan, the artist who was a mentor to Sottsass from his student days in the 1930s, until his death in 1958. It was Spazzapan who ignited Sottsass's passionate preoccupation with colour. More fundamentally it was because of Spazzapan that Sottsass struggled to understand for some years if he was actually an artist rather than an architect. He painted, he made sculpture, and took part in a number of significant group shows in the 1940s, while at the same time practising architecture both with his father and on his own account. When he stopped painting, he wrote in 1965 that: 'a painter has a more sudden, intense and dramatic perception, for instance, of colour. A painter does not think of colour, he's inside it. I am more capable of spreading colours in space, than on a piece of paper.'

Colour was the key preoccupation of Sottsass's artistic life. Long after they parted, one of Sottsass's former partners, the British designer James Irvine, remembers discussing the precise colour that Sottsass wanted for a project. Sottsass never used the scientific conventions that usually define colour. Instead he told Irvine that he wanted to match the shade of a dress that he remembered Pivano wearing at a party a decade before. Would he, Sottsass asked Irvine, go to her apartment and ask her if she still had it? Irvine went and talked to her, and Pivano duly lent the dress.

Throughout his long career, Sottsass always described himself as an architect. He was trained as one, he was proud of his work as an architect and he speculated about architecture for the whole of his life. 'When I was born, my father who was an architect, put a pencil in my hands. He wanted me to become an architect too. With that pencil he was trying to set in motion the destiny he had planned for me.'

But it is arguable that what Sottsass did was not architecture in the way that it is conventionally defined in the modern world. He was an architect in the sense that he enjoyed the myth of architecture. He had been fascinated by the ancient Vedic Sanskrit traditions of India ever since he first visited the subcontinent. Proportion and space play an essential part in Veda ritual. To be an architect is to be an archetype, as it is to be a warrior or a priest, unlike being an industrial designer, which has only been a distinct category since mass production sliced through the intimate connection between user and maker.

Architecture is a profession that has existed in every civilization. But in the twentieth century it became a commodity. Sottsass resisted that tendency. He tried to make authentic architecture. To do so, he needed the help of others.

When he was a young man it was his father. During the most successful period of his architectural career in the 1980s, it was the support of American Johanna Grawunder, who joined his studio in Milan in 1985.

What attracted Sottsass was the idea of architecture as one of the most fundamental forms of creativity, rather than the more pallid architectural discourse of his time. He accepted that he was not in fact an artist. And having done so, he liked the idea of being an architect better than being defined as a designer, no matter how gifted. Sottsass's architecture was a series of intense highly personal spatial experiments that stood almost entirely outside the architectural conversation of their time.

Sottsass made buildings that consisted of boxes within boxes, and spaces inside spaces. They were exercises in using form, surface, texture and colour to create an emotional impact. If his architecture has any parallels it is in the work of Aldo Rossi, the architect who defined the landscape of Italian architecture in the 1980s, with his preoccupation with archetypal forms. His industrial design on the one hand, and his furniture on the other had affected the climate in which every designer of his time worked.

Other than in the formal honorific way that Italy still reserves for its professionals — *dottore, avvocato, architetto* and so on — it was not as an architect that others defined him. It was an omission that disturbed and irritated him. Like many Italian architects it was as a designer that Sottsass established his international reputation, but it was through architecture that he did his best to express himself. It was not a paradox that he could resolve easily.

One of the most characteristic of Sottsass's industrial projects was intimately connected with both colour and with storytelling. In the revolutionary year of 1968, when Sottsass convinced Olivetti to manufacture a portable typewriter with a bright red body, named the 'Valentine', he suggested that this was a machine that was designed to keep poets company on lonely weekends in the country. Lonely was a word that Sottsass used about himself a lot. He would often suggest that he had no friends and that he did not feel at home anywhere. Almost from the start of his career, he had worked for both Giorgio and Gianni Agnelli and a little later, the Olivetti family — the very heart of the Italian business establishment — but he never felt part of it. He knew the design world intimately, but never wanted to be defined or limited by it. Sottsass enjoyed dressing stylishly; he enjoyed the sun and wine. But he could also withdraw into melancholia. Radice would sometimes find him at home in the late afternoon, coiled up in a foetal position.

Sottsass designed his typewriter to slide into an extruded plastic carrying case, like a bucket. The case could, he suggested, become a makeshift stool should the urge to use the typewriter overwhelm the poet in the midst of a natural landscape. Perry King, Sottsass's English assistant who worked with him on the design of the machine, has suggested that the decision to embellish each typewriter spool with an orange plastic lid, with a circular tip at its centre, was intended to be a suggestion of a nipple, contrasting in colour with the body of the machine in the manner of one of Tom Wesselmann's Great American Nudes. It's a reference that is just subliminal enough not to be offensive.

What makes the Valentine such a fascinating object, even now, two or three decades after the digital explosion that has made all typewriters as arcane and technologically redundant as a wind-up gramophone, is that it was one of the first examples of a machine given shape by a designer driven by an understanding of the emotional nature of the relationship between people and the things that they use in daily life.

In the narrow sense of the meaning of the word 'function', there was no functional purpose to the colour of the Valentine, or to those orange nipples. But Sottsass understood that to place a red machine on a desk would be to create a presence in a room entirely different from one that was coloured gunmetal grey, the conventional hue for office equipment at the time. He knew that his typewriter would be perceived differently, used differently and understood, consciously or not, as belonging to an entirely different category of object.

He expended as much creative energy on the form of the case as he did on the machine itself. He wanted to understand what it would be like to carry it, how it would look and feel, swinging against the body. Case and machine were designed to work together, as well as individually. Unusually, the carrying handle is hinged to the top of the machine itself, not fixed to the case. When in use, the handle protrudes through a slot in the case, which in turn is held in place by two black rubber straps terminating in crosses that stop them from coming unintentionally undone. The finish of the plastic used for the machine is glossy and smooth. The case, chamfered to reduce its apparent bulk, has a matt textured finish — implying a hint of leather grain, as if it were a briefcase.

The plastic housing is sculpted to wrap seamlessly around the mechanical parts of the machine. The plastic elements are strong, simple forms. They are as distinctive as they are tactile, encouraging you to touch them. But Sottsass's idea of simplifying the mechanism by omitting lower-case characters and dropping the bell to make it cheaper, proved too much for Olivetti. They saw themselves as radical, but not that radical.

It's a machine that retains meaning even after it has lost its practical use. I have one in my study, and I am unlikely ever to use it to type a letter, or to write a book. Yet it is still an object that has an emotional resonance without actually being used for the purpose for which it was intended. It offers an insight into the way that design can give an object a personality. It reflects a very particular moment, the high point of the glossy plastic era of the 1960s. But in one respect it also provided a precedent that was followed many years later by Apple, which suddenly transformed the desktop computer in a similar way. Using a mix of transparent plastic and acid-sharp citrus colours — memorably described by Steve Jobs as delicious enough to lick — the iMac created a new model for the computer, one that signalled that it was playful, knowing and sensuous, rather than technocratic and businesslike.

The Valentine is an object that says a lot about Sottsass and about his passion for colour. It demonstrates his imagination and his ability to take a humble everyday object churned out in tens of thousands by factory workers and give it an identity. It reflects Sottsass's life-long exploration of the tension between the ostensible commercial purpose of an industrial object, and its ability to be shaped in such a way as to call into question the values and the culture of the society that brought it into being.

The Valentine was about the idea of portability, of the lightweight, of the freedom that it gave its owner to work not just away from the desk and the office, or the home, but outside. Of course it wasn't actually that portable; there is a lot of heavy metal inside the red plastic casing. You wouldn't want to carry it too far, but it did anticipate the idea of being able to take work anywhere that the digital explosion was one day going to make possible. When the decoupling of work from the office eventually did take place, it turned out to be anything but the liberation that Sottsass envisaged. The constant connection with the Internet has made us free from office hours, but the slaves of always being available. I acquired my Valentine, in a red version rather than the deep blue, olive green or ivory versions, long after the Olivetti factory in Barcelona that made it from 1969 closed. It sits on my shelf as a reminder of a time when technology was both more innocent and more knowing than it is now.

Sottsass himself had an uneasy relationship with his creation. Towards the end of his life, he lost patience during an interview:

I worked 60 years of my life, and it seems the only thing
I did is this fucking red machine. And it came out a mistake.
It was supposed to be a very inexpensive portable, to
sell in the market, like pens. It only had capital letters,
it didn't have a bell. I wanted the case to be inexpensive.
Then the people at Olivetti said you cannot sell this kind
of cheap Chinese thing. So, everything was put back:
the lower-case letters, the bell, even the expensive plastic,
which I was thinking should be this horrible, cheap plastic.
So, it was a mistake.

The day of that interview was cold and Sottsass, who was eighty-eight at the time, was in some pain from a back problem that made it difficult for him to travel, but his mind was as sharp as ever.

He might well have been even more irritated to have worked for all those years and be remembered only for the astonishing scene on Milan's Corso Europa one night in September 1981 when he launched the Memphis movement, his onslaught on conventional ideas of what constituted good design that ignited the design world like wildfire. There were a thousand people in the street trying to get into the showroom, the scene looking more like a nightclub than a crucial moment in the history of twentieth-century design.

Ettore Sottsass had many careers. He was an architect, a photographer and artist, a writer, an editor, a reluctant soldier and a designer. He was a football enthusiast. When he came back from the war, he and his father would go to watch Juventus, one of Turin's two local teams. After the match they would go home on the tram for spaghetti with tomato but no basil.

If he liked them, he talked about women as having sad eyes. He talked about men as being calm, if he liked *them*. He himself certainly had the sad, grave eyes of a bloodhound, a man touched by the melancholia of his Austrian heritage, the sad eyes of a man who had seen more of life than perhaps he really wanted to. He wasn't always calm. He was capable of unpredictable and explosive bursts of impatience at what he took to be the stupidity of others. He was fascinated by those people who had something to offer creatively and gave them every freedom to do their own work in their own way in his studio. But those who he didn't respect and in whom he wasn't interested were invisible to him. James Irvine, who worked with Sottsass for almost a decade, told me he could be dangerous to work for. 'Try too much to be like him, and you are lost. To work for him, and to survive, you had to develop your own voice.'

Architects are notoriously ungenerous about each other. Every job, no matter how small, that they lose to another architect causes them real pain. Yet when Sottsass felt that he had designed enough stores and offices for Esprit, the Californian fashion retailer that underpinned his studio for much of the 1980s, he introduced Doug Tompkins, Esprit's owner, to Antonio Citterio, an architect that he hardly knew but thought was in need of some work.

Sottsass lived an extraordinary life that began in Innsbruck where he was born as a citizen of the Austro-Hungarian Empire, and ended in Milan on the last day of the year in 2007, with the comfort of a Buddhist monk, summoned to his bedside by Radice. He was cremated without a formal religious ceremony. Instead his friends came to the modest apartment near the Piazza Castello that he had shared with Barbara to say goodbye. His body was laid out, his hands clasped together. He looked so peaceful and composed that the doctor who had pronounced him dead returned for a second, closer look.

He was a man whose life reflected the course of modern Italian history and who made us think about the material world around us differently. Without him, the world would have been a different and a poorer place.

Childhood

19

Ettore Sottsass was born in Innsbruck in the autumn of 1917. The town sits on the edge of the Brenner Pass — the threshold between Teutonic and Latin Europe, and the division between two equally unsatisfactory national stereotypes of discipline and indulgence. At that time the pass was still a connection between the two halves of the Tyrol, and did not yet mark an international frontier. It was the link between Sottsass's mother — Antonia Peintner from Hall, a medieval walled town near Innsbruck, in the German-speaking north, who would have called herself an Austrian, or perhaps even a German — and Sottsass's father, also called Ettore Sottsass, who was from the ancient town of Cembra in the Trentino in the Italian-speaking south, and who was as proud to identify himself as an Italian as one day his son would be. The Tyrol was a sliver of Europe that over the centuries had passed through many hands. It had once been an independent duchy, then a bishopric. After that it was part of the Austro-Hungarian Empire, apart from a brief period when it was taken over by Bavaria. Much like the polyglot Swiss Confederation immediately to the west, it had retained a sense of itself as a distinct and, despite its linguistic diversity, cohesive entity. The landscape, the mountain light, the weather and the elements of a shared architectural vernacular — characterized by stone and timber farmhouses, and in the towns by more elaborate buildings whose facades were embellished with ornamental patterns worked into plaster — all served to link north with south.

Italian unification in the mid-nineteenth century had triggered a wave of agitation in the Italian speakers in the towns of the Trentino to secede from the Empire, and to join the new kingdom to the south. Politics remained intense in the region throughout the twentieth century. Benito Mussolini, while he was still a socialist journalist, worked briefly in the city of Trento to rally local support for the cause of Italian national unity — although he soon judged it expedient to return to Italy to avoid the attention of the Austrian secret police. Later, in the 1960s, a group of radicals at the University of Trento established the first Red Brigades terrorist cell. Italy's decision to fight alongside the Western Allies in World War I, rather than with the Central powers, was made in pursuit of its claims on Austrian territories. With the collapse of the Austro-Hungarian Empire, the province of South Tyrol and the city of Trieste were handed over to Italy following the Treaty of Versailles in 1919. Italian irredentist ambitions did not stop there; the posturing poet-turned-warlord Gabriele D'Annunzio seized the port city that is called Rijeka today, and held it hostage under the name of Fiume, for almost two years.

The Brenner Pass had been the link between northern and southern Europe since Roman times. For the Austro-Hungarian Empire, it was an essential link to its southern provinces, but the imperial attitude to the area and its citizens was ambivalent. Italian speakers were not as disadvantaged in Austro-Hungary as the Croats, for example, or the Slovenes. But Italians were lower down the social scale than those citizens who had German as their mother tongue. Sottsass's father, an officer in the Imperial army and a successful architect, was well aware of this fact and he made himself as much at home in German as he was in Italian. After elementary school, his education was conducted entirely in German. His diplomas, his textbooks and his class work are all German. Perhaps as a result, he became an ardent supporter of the union of the Trentino with the Italian fatherland.

The family name was rendered differently at the time that Sottsass junior was born. It was Sot Sas then, or sometimes Sot-Sas; Trentino dialect for 'under the stone', and also the name of a mountain hamlet with which the family may once have had a connection. The hyphen came and went, as if in compensation for the addition of the extra 't'.

Giovanni Battista Sottsass, Ettore Sottsass's paternal grandfather, had a road building business with a gang of labourers working for him. Their job was to construct and maintain the routes down through the peaks of the Dolomites across to the Adige plain and the deep valley of Cembra. It was tough, physically demanding work for both gang and gang master. After an early morning spent blasting rock with dynamite, breakfast for *nonno* Sottsass was a wooden bowl of glutinous tripe, taken with a flask of throat-burning grappa.

Giovanni's wife Rosina gave birth to their son, Ettore Sottsass senior in Nave San Rocco on 12 April 1892. As he grew up, the boy moved from school to school. He went from Cavalese to Predazzo, and then to Lana d'Adige as his father's work took him from place to place. Giovanni Sottsass eventually made enough money to send his son to school in Trento, and then to support his studies at the trade school in Innsbruck where he took a diploma in building. There are surviving drawings of considerable accomplishment that show his technical studies of the intricacies of reinforcing steel. Beautifully rendered in watercolour, they demonstrate his grasp of technical as well as aesthetic issues. Sottsass senior was able to turn what he had learned from his father's skills as a road builder into the foundation of his own career and, with this underpinning, he eventually moved up the social scale to become a professional.

Sottsass senior was apprenticed to August Fingerle, a well-regarded architect with a practice in Bolzano (or Bozen, as its German-speaking residents call it) that had an aristocratic clientele — Fingerle was commissioned by the last Russian ambassador to the Emperor to design a villa in the mountains. Sottsass senior met his wife while he was in Bolzano. Antonia Peintner was, as her son later described her, a fair-haired Austrian known as Nina. She was one of eight children, and Sottsass junior had six aunts and one uncle, Oscar. Nina's father was a master carpenter who specialized in making domestic furniture and in the carving of baroque-style altarpieces, and he executed his future son-in-law's first furniture designs.

To become an architect in his own right, Sottsass senior needed a professional qualification. The best place to get it was Vienna, the capital of the Empire of which he was a provincial citizen. The city had two schools of architecture. The larger of them, at the Polytechnic Institute, sidestepped the 'artistic' aspects of architecture, and had a relatively open admissions policy. The Akademie der bildenden Künste (Academy of Fine Arts) was more demanding — students had to be at least twenty, and to demonstrate artistic as well as technical ability in a highly competitive exam. Less than a dozen students were accepted each year, but Sottsass's father showed the exceptional promise needed to secure a place. He set off for the great metropolis in 1912, on a train that would take him 400 miles east.

As a student, Sottsass senior sported a wing collar, a frock coat with a waistcoat, a carefully knotted silk tie, a broad-brimmed felt hat and a dashing moustache. He was a young man, eager not to be taken for a provincial, and equally determined to learn all that he could from Vienna.

In the first decade and a half of the twentieth century, Vienna, rather than London, Paris or Berlin, was the place that Modernism as an aesthetic ideology was born. A wave of building at the turn of the century crystallized new techniques and a new sensibility. With Otto Wagner, Josef Hoffmann, Adolf Loos and Jože Plečnik all active in the years leading up to World War I, Vienna's new architecture was the most creatively charged in Europe. And while Wagner and his followers reshaped the buildings of Vienna, Sigmund

Freud developed a new understanding of the mind. Gustav Mahler was at the height of his powers. Gustav Klimt and Egon Schiele challenged expectations of art and its subject matter. Robert Musil embarked on his career as a writer that culminated in his unfinished novel *The Man Without Qualities*, a devastating critique of the imperial system.

Optimistic readings of history associate creative leaps with the idea of economic and social progress, but this flowering of Viennese culture took place in the last days of an Empire that was on the edge of cataclysmic destruction. Sottsass's father was shaped decisively by his experience of pre-war Vienna and Sottsass himself can be understood as the product of its faint afterglow.

Otto Wagner got his chance to rebuild the city when Karl Lueger, the mayor whose appointment Emperor Franz Josef I at first refused to confirm, despite his victory at the polls in three separate elections, finally took power. The Emperor believed that Lueger and the anti-Semitism of his Christian Social Party would fatally damage Austro-Hungary. Despite the imperial misgivings, Lueger finally took control of the city in 1897. He set about a modernizing agenda to deal with a population explosion. Municipal gas, water, transport and electricity systems were introduced, or upgraded. Vienna developed a social welfare policy and began to plan new parks and civic spaces. It was in Lueger's time that Vienna saw the building of Österreichische Postsparkasse (Austrian Post Office Savings Bank) and the metro stations that Wagner designed.

The Sparkasse, Wagner's masterpiece, was completed five years before Sottsass's father arrived in Vienna. With its rooftop maidens cast from aluminium, laurel wreaths held high over their heads, its banking hall with a milky glass vaulted ceiling and distinctive chairs with their legs protected by chaste metal socks, the building was the world's first monument to Modernism. There was nothing else like it. Its grid of tiny aluminium studs set into a screen of stone cladding served to reveal the masonry facade for what it was — a skin, rather than a self-supporting structure. Wagner also designed the Steinhof, Vienna's vast hospital for the mentally ill, a site he crowned with an extraordinary domed church, its interior lined with white glazed ceramic tiles, designed to console its inmates. (Some years later, Sottsass's cousin from his mother's side, Max Peintner, wrote one of the earliest modern monographs on Wagner.)

Wagner was to have as important an impact on architectural education as he had on the face of Vienna. In 1894, he became the Professor of Architecture at the city's Academy of Fine Arts, and he promptly set out to establish it as a training ground for talented young architects, capable of responding to the emerging modern world. His inaugural address was published under the title *Modern Architecture*, which remained in print as a textbook long after Wagner had left the Academy, and its principles continued to shape the course under Friedrich Ohmann, who succeeded Wagner in 1904.

Sottsass senior had read Wagner's intimidating but inspiring inaugural address (his son kept his father's copy), in which he cautioned his students that it would take more than his teaching to turn them into architects:

> After your academic studies you must still spend several years in an atelier. And you must educate yourselves through travel before your can confront on your own the solution of problems.
> Our path of life is troublesome and full of thorns, but it is also the most beautiful. Someone before me has said that the architect with this happy combination of idealism and realism is the crowning glory of modern man, but I add that his creative and productive nature must elevate him far above the level of the ordinary.

It was an ambition that inspired Sottsass senior, and one that he would later be determined to pass on to his son. Wagner continued:

> Two things must be *innate* to you, taste and imagination. Assiduous study and experience must join these facilities if you are to develop into the architects that the present time demands. To achieve this goal, my efforts will not be lacking, but I ask you not to think that I am capable of making each of you an architect. It takes a natural ability, the mastery of preliminary studies, a strong will, a certain independence and the experience of a lifetime for the sown seed to mature into fruit.

Wagner was determined to produce a school of architecture with a modern approach. He would not countenance students comfortable to be mere revivalists, or 'copyists' as he described them.

Contrary to the view of my immediate predecessors, I am of the opinion that only a few truly talented architects should have the benefit of the training at this school. Architectural hermaphrodites simply cannot be expected to nurture much of a burning desire for architecture. As a teacher, I also have the duty to show everyone the right path, and I hope in this way to reduce in our profession at least somewhat, the number of dreary types who have misspent their lives. Therefore do not judge me too harshly when I make a rather meticulous selection among the students presented to me. Rest assured that I am acting solely in the interest of the school, the profession, and art.

Students were expected to spend their first year concentrating on a single project. Wagner told his students that it would:

... probably be the first task that you will face when you enter into professional life, namely, a simple Viennese apartment house. I intend by this to make you rather proficient, first and foremost, in construction and the understanding of needs. If, as is most likely, enough time is left, you can then proceed to the solution of the 'individual dwelling'...

Wagner's successor Ohmann was a distinguished architect in his own right, with a practice throughout the Empire, working in a style that could broadly be understood as following Wagner's lead, though with a particular sensitivity to the traditions of the cities in which he worked. He built the Hotel Central in Prague while he was a professor at the Academy of Applied Art there, as well as the Archaeological Museum in Split in Croatia. He was also responsible for completing many of the civic improvements initiated by Wagner in Vienna. He designed bridges, viaducts and embankments, and was in charge of work at the city's royal palaces — designing the palm house in Vienna's Burggarten.

In 1912, the year that Sottsass's father arrived in Vienna, Ohmann began building an imposing set of assembly rooms in Meran, the spa town in South Tyrol in which Sottsass senior would build a new town hall when the area was being Italianized into Merano in the 1920s.

Josef Hoffmann and Adolf Loos, Wagner's two most gifted successors, continued to build on his achievements. The controversy over Loos's 1910 Goldman & Salatsch building, regarded by some as insultingly blunt to its neighbour, the Hofburg (the Imperial palace), was still alive in 1912. Hoffmann, teaching at Vienna's other design school, the Universität für angewandte Kunst (University of Applied Art), was working on the Palais Stoclet in Brussels. He joined the Vienna Secession with Koloman Moser and Joseph Maria Olbrich, a group of younger artists and designers who left the more traditional artists' academy in 1897. Hoffmann was also responsible for establishing the Wiener Werkstätte, manufacturing exquisite pieces of furniture and decorative objects, distinguished by a refined geometry and rectilinear pattern making. The Werkstätte and the Secession had a clear impact on the work of Sottsass's father. It would inspire his professional career after the war. And when Ettore junior was born, he designed his son's cot, and embellished his family photograph album in a style that clearly reflects the Secessionist aesthetic.

Sottsass senior's studies were interrupted by the outbreak of World War I. He was called up to fight for Austria in August 1914, before Italy entered the war and there was no real question of conflicted loyalties. Lieutenant Sottsass fought in the campaign to stop the Russian advance into Galicia. He was wounded badly enough to be sent home to recuperate in the following spring. But even after Italy entered the war, Sottsass's father continued to fight on the side of the enemies of what he saw as his real country. With a German-speaking wife he would have had conflicted loyalties between Austria and Italy, but for a man of his background he had no real choice but to obey the call of the military authorities in Vienna.

Sottsass's parents were married just before Christmas in 1916. The ceremony took place in Cembra, in the church of San Pietro, a handsome structure with Romanesque origins and a stone tower, topped by a steeple. There is Gothic tracery, an apse, and a sixteenth-century fresco cycle painted on the ceiling of the crypt. (Albrecht Dürer passed through Cembra on his way south to Venice 500 years before. He stayed in the castle of Segonzano and went to see the curious rock formations carved out by millennia of erosion, locally known as the pyramids. His watercolours record the Val de Cembra and the tower of San Pietro.) The wedding took place with snow on the ground. Sottsass's father wore his army greatcoat with two ranks of brass buttons marching across his chest and his military kepi. His mother left the church in a cape coat with a fur collar, a fox muff and a rakish tricorn hat. The ceremony was, as his parents later wrote in the family album, 'simple and without pretension but it was a reflection of the good hearts of country people'. There was a brief honeymoon in Cembra and Innsbruck, during which their only child was conceived. Sottsass's father went back to the war immediately afterwards.

The son of Antonia and Ettore was born in Innsbruck on 14 September 1917 in what he would later say was a house on the Sterngasse, an address that he translated as 'the alley of the stars'. Perhaps there was such a street in 1917, but it is not in today's Innsbruck street directory. Sottsass's mother gave their child his father's name to keep his memory alive, should he not return from the ever-bloodier war that was still raging.

After the birth of their son, her husband was sent to the Dolomite front, to fight in the brutal conflict between Italy and Austro-Hungary on Mount Pasubio. For two years imperial troops built the tunnels that still honeycomb the mountains. They were designed to allow the Austrians to keep their outposts resupplied without coming under fire but also to extend under the Italian lines and use mines to destroy them. The Italians responded by digging their own tunnels in an attempt to keep up with the Austrians, and to threaten them with landmines of their own. Thousands were killed fighting in conditions of terrible cold at the most demanding altitudes. Despite the sacrifice, there were no breakthroughs.

While his father was away fighting, Sottsass and his mother lived with his Austrian grandparents in a wooden house in Wilten, on the edge of Innsbruck. The young Sottsass's first words were in German. '*Wie schöne*' ('How pretty') he said, pointing his finger. It was 1918; and he had just seen his first candlelit Christmas tree. In *Scritto di Notte*, his picaresque autobiography, Sottsass suggests that it was the first documented example of his habit of offering gratuitous and unsolicited aesthetic advice.

Sottsass junior carried the smells and tastes of his childhood with him for the rest of his long life. His Austrian grandparents lived in a wooden house — more of a barn than a house — that stood close beside a railway viaduct. Sottsass remembered the flavour of the minestrone that his grandmother cooked, the soup that she made with burnt flour, with pinches of cumin and potato scraps. He remembered his mother's father, 'the honest, serious carver of poor saints, saying a quiet grace for the food when it arrived on the family's table'. He remembered the dumplings that one of his aunts made, full of sugar and apricots. 'She put sugar in the pasta too. In the mountains, where everything was a bit dry, a bit salty, there were only acid mountain berries, it's a custom of mountain people who need something sweet to put sugar in dumplings.' He remembers living in a house that was made entirely of wood. He remembered the special scent of wood polish and how his mother and his aunts scrubbed the floor every week with soap and water. He didn't recall the event itself, but he remembered being told that he had been found asleep in his cradle with a crushed mouse clutched in his hand. It was the cradle that his father had designed, and that his grandfather had made for him.

Whether those tastes and smells really go back to the first two years of the life that Sottsass spent at his grandparents, or are memories of the regular visits that he and his mother made after the war, when it had become another country, is unclear. But it is not hard to see the effect on Sottsass's adulthood of an early life as the only male child in a house full of adoring women. He remembered the home that he and his parents finally settled in after the war also by its smells. The family lived on the edge of Trento in a house built for employees of the local construction department that came with the job. The house, on two floors, was just one hundred metres from the railway line that went from Verona up to the Brenner Pass.

Sottsass recalled the scent of engine oil, coal, smoke and burnt grass. He also described the vinegary aroma of an abandoned sauerkraut factory across the road.

It was in the house in Trento that he had his first suggestion of an erotic experience. As a ten-year-old, a girl even younger than him asked him for a place in which she could use the lavatory. He took her into the house, showed her a dark corner and turned his back. Amid the scent of the wood and of cooking smells coming from the kitchen, it was a Proustian moment that left him, he said, with a life-long association between sensuality and food. After smell, touch and taste, Sottsass's other abiding memories are of sound. At home as a child, in the mountains as a youth and in the army during the war, song was always an accompaniment to his life.

With the war over, and the Trentino now part of the Kingdom of Italy, his father's hopes of unification with the Italian fatherland had come true — even if he had risked his life in the fight against it. He had been forced by the call-up to leave Vienna without completing his studies, but Ohmann, his professor, signed Sottsass's father's diploma in 1918 anyway. He took his family south through the Brenner, to start a new life. He got a job with the civil administration in the newly Italianized province of Trentino, working to make good the damage done by four years of war. The family moved around a great deal in the early years. They lived by the railway line in Trento, in the Villa Prada on the edge of the town. At the end of November 1919 they left for Pieve Tesino, where they were based for the next couple of years. Sottsass senior was in charge of its reconstruction as well as that of its neighbouring settlements. The family lived in two rooms rented from the mayor.

The family left Pieve in the autumn of 1921 for Borgo Valsugana, where Sottsass believed he would find more culturally ambitious work. They lived in a barn that had once been a storeroom for the fire brigade and where they needed to put up partitions to separate bedroom from kitchen. Sottsass's father was determined to take on a more creative architectural role, and to make the transition from the pragmatic world of engineering into the kind of architecture that he had been educated for. The family returned to Pieve, where Sottsass's father took part in a competition for a group of low-cost homes in Trento. His design came second, but the jury's original decision was overturned. Sottsass senior's proposal was later judged to be the only one that could be executed within the budget, and so he got the job that would be the real start of his architectural career.

By this stage Sottsass had already been infected by his father's passion for design and started to draw. There is a surviving sketch he made when he was still not six years old, that suggests a sophisticated sensibility in its attempts to depict space and not just flat facades in the way of most naïve drawings. Sottsass's future as a designer began to take concrete shape with the drawings he started producing at the age of five or six in order to 'leave a mark on the emptiness of the blank page... the way primitive man might have incised lines or dots on the bones of whales or heaven knows what other animals a long, long, long time ago'. For Sottsass, 'signs and symbols' became 'an obsession that pursued me — and has continued to pursue me all my life'.

Sottsass was fascinated by his father, who worked from home at that time, using pencils, Indian ink, crayons and brushes to sketch his designs on large sheets of tracing paper. 'I would watch my father doing a kind of silent ballet as he made his marks... for me he turned into a special man, one who was different from all other men.'

Antonia 'Nina' Peintner devoted herself to her only child. She made his clothes, finding inspiration in fashion magazines she bought from Austria. When she walked him to the gate of the Pietro Pedrotti elementary school in the autumn of 1922 (the same school that his father had attended two decades earlier) Sottsass cut something of a dash in a stylish sailor suit.

They moved again to the second floor of a new villa, on Via Ottaviano Rovereti in Trento, and Sottsass enrolled at the Giuseppe Verdi elementary school. The villa had a little orchard and a garden behind it. His father designed the furniture for the dining room, and had it made in red wood. He designed Sottsass's bed, which was lacquered in white and lit by a batik lampshade, decorated with crowns of small bells, roses, heart-shaped leaves, blue flowers from the fields and all those things in the taste of the Secession. In the album that they gave their son, its cover also embellished in Secessionist style embroidery, a lock of Sottsass's very fair hair is preserved inside the cover. The same album records his first moments, his first steps and even his first teacher, 'Gius Sief, a good hearted soul from the mountains'. Sottsass remembered his white beard, and his other teacher, a plump woman.

In *Scritto di Notte*, Sottsass wrote:

My parents never said to me if I was, or was not intelligent.
When I was very little I lived in the mountains, and in
the midst of those big mountains the problem of intelligence
didn't seem to matter. I spent those fantastic early
childhood years in forests of towering spruce and larch
with greyish beard lichen hanging from them, looking
for blueberries and cranberries and yellow and brown
mushrooms that grew on the ground or were hidden
beneath the moss and the mildewed layers of fallen pine
needles — the detritus of countless rainy autumns. [...]
The world was made up of animals, mountains, butterflies,
birds, clouds, lakes, rocks and flowers, and every single
thing had its own colour; every single thing stood out
because of its colour; every single thing was what it was,
with its particular colour.

Both of Sottsass's grandfathers worked with their hands, and Sottsass too was always able to make toys, mechanisms and models. Sottsass's father joined the Circolo Artistico Tridentino, the most active cultural group in the area at the time. He showed his work in its exhibitions and publications, and at the exhibition of Modern Art held in Trento in 1924. He made a number of sketches to design memorials to the fallen of World War I. Two of them were realized, one at Pinzolo and the other at Calceranica al Lago. These are extraordinary objects: simple stone slabs in village churchyards and cemeteries, under the protection of stone roofs, supported by stone columns at each corner, but with jagged, carved edges. They look like close cousins of the work Sottsass junior would go on to make six decades later. They are about the essentials of shelter and making a mark in time and place, in materials that belong where they are, and yet without specific architectural language.

Sottsass senior's architectural career had three distinct phases that took him from reconstruction of the damage done to the Trentino by the fighting in World War I to the post-war rebuilding of Italy in the 1940s, by way of his work in the 1930s after he moved to Turin, where he embraced the vocabulary of the rationalism that was the Italian form of Modernism.

His first serious architectural works were clearly influenced by Ohmann, who was gradually moving away from an early interest in Art Nouveau to a rediscovery of more classical forms. Ohmann was nevertheless careful to look for roots in local traditions and inflections, a reflection of the sensitivities of Austro-Hungary, an imperial system that survived for as long as it did by creating a national identity that was larger than any of its constituent parts.

Sottsass senior's work from this period is captured in a number of remarkably elaborate and richly coloured renderings. There was more to it than an explosion of decorative detail; Ohmann taught his students to explore the possibilities of new construction techniques. He gave Sottsass's father the architectural language that shaped his early buildings. When Sottsass senior returned to the Trentino, it was his time with Ohmann that helped him to look for clues in the vernacular of the region to form the starting point for his own work, and the means to give it a contemporary expression.

His career as an architect was progressing, as he moved from reconstruction to designing buildings on an increasing scale throughout the Trentino. The architectural conversation was changing — just as the Italian political context was changing. With the coming to power of Mussolini, the state was seeking to present itself as an authoritative, forward-looking, modernizing force. A new generation of Italian architects was responding to the sobriety of the German and Dutch schools to come up with a particularly Italian form of Modernism. In Como there was Giuseppe Terragni. In Turin, Giuseppe Pagano — an architect who like Sottsass's father had been born an Austro-Hungarian citizen, but who had been committed enough to the Italian cause to flee conscription into the Austrian army and to fight on the Italian side, before studying at Turin's Polytechnic. And in Rome there was Adalberto Libera.

The conviction of their designs brought about a decisive shift in Sottsass's own work. While he was still finishing the town hall in Merano — which, though it was built as part of the Italianization of this predominantly German-speaking town, was a dignified exercise in classically inspired contextualism — he won a competition in 1928 to design a lido complex in Bolzano with a local collaborator named Willy Weyhenmeyer.

The project marked his first break with his Viennese architectural education. The lido was a striking complex of buildings on a conspicuous site. It celebrated the cult of the outdoors shared by all authoritarian regimes and its generous facilities were intended to demonstrate to Bolzano's recalcitrant German-speakers the benefits of their newly-acquired compulsory Italian citizenship. There would undoubtedly be more opportunities for architects that had the regime's support to repeat that lesson. Unlike his previous work, this was a strictly ordered composition, based on a regular geometric facade, bold gestures and clearly expressed distinct forms stripped of ornament.

It was a project that gave Sottsass senior his chance to leave rural Italy. Sottsass's father had a connection with an engineer in Turin named Galdini. It was in conversation with him that Sottsass had the idea of moving the family to Turin. Galdini talked up the opportunities that Turin could offer and the possibilities that they would have of working together. Sottsass's father went to see the city. Things did not look as promising as Galdini had suggested, but he decided to make the move anyway — delaying long enough to find somewhere for his family to live in Turin and a school for his son, where Sottsass junior started in October 1929. The Galdini connection failed to live up to Sottsass's expectations. There is a plaintive note in the family album, addressed to their son that records: 'On 3 October, 1929, we left Trento for Turin. The Galdini family, the only people that we knew there, turned out to be insincere false friends.'

The wedding of Ettore Sottsass senior
and Antonia Peintner, 1916

1920

Ettore Sottsass, 1920

Turin, 1939

With the Monterosa Division,
Tuscany, 1944

Tuscany, 1965

Ivrea, 1968

Milan, 1967

Ridgway, Colorado, USA, 1987

Milan, 2002

Turin

35

The Sottsass family decided to pack up and leave Trento and the mountains for Turin not because they had to, but because the city offered the prospect of a better education for the young Ettore Sottsass and a wider range of architectural work for his father. Sottsass senior was only thirty-seven, and his career in the Trentino was far from over. He was still working on remodelling the town hall in Merano, and he had recently won the competition to build the lido in Bolzano. He had been born in the mountains and he loved them. He was an enthusiastic skier, but for a man who had studied in Vienna and had read Otto Wagner's advice to his students, Trento could not provide the same creative challenge as Turin, or the sense of being at the centre of things rather than on the periphery. He had to move on if he was going to realize what he saw as his potential.

Turin was once the capital city of the Duchy of Savoy, then of the Kingdom of Sardinia, and finally, if briefly, of the whole of Italy. It was a city in which *haute bourgeois* young women would be presented as debutantes at court in the spectacular great hall of the Palazzo Madama in their coming-out season. It was a city of piano lessons at the conservatoire, and grand cafés full of gold leaf, cut-glass mirrors and filigree, filled by newspapermen, opera singers and professors. It was a city equipped with an improbable number of monuments to King Vittorio Emanuele II, founding father of a united nation. They existed in order to convince their makers that unification had finally triumphed, and that Italy could at last take its place among Europe's modern nation states. Its centre was a genteel, modestly scaled court city, just big enough to support the bureaucracy of state craft: a ministry of war, a treasury, a foreign service. The city was not a microscopic ducal fiefdom like Siena or Urbino, but it was not exactly Paris or Vienna either.

Turin at the start of the twentieth century still had a claim to being the most modern city in Italy on the basis of its progressive tradition of scientific research. It was in an area that produced two remarkable industrial giants, Fiat in Turin itself and Olivetti just thirty miles away in Ivrea. Fiat still dominates the manufacturing landscape of Italy, but Olivetti has vanished, leaving behind the painfully empty, lost industrial utopia of Ivrea, the company town that no longer has a company.

In Turin, Fiat's Lingotto complex (opened in 1923) was an extraordinary summation of industrial architecture, running straight as an engineer could make it for more than a third of a kilometre, topped by a rooftop test track with spiral concrete access ramps at either end. It looked as if it owed more to the over-heated rhetoric of Futurism than to pragmatic business sense, yet it was the cornerstone of Italy's capitalist economy.

The possibility that Turin was already at the start of a long decline was not yet apparent when the Sottsass family moved down from the mountains. The year before their arrival, the city had staged a national exposition in the royal gardens, the Parco del Valentino. It was an event that gave the ambitious and talented architectural prodigy Giuseppe Pagano a chance to make his mark as its technical director. He designed several pavilions, and worked on some of the exhibitions. But the most startling looking project in the park, the Futurist Pavilion, had nothing to do with Pagano. Designed by Enrico Prampolini, it was a huge, sculptural object of jagged geometries that stood five storeys high, ringed by projecting stairways that seemed to belong to an entirely different world from the one inhabited by the crowds of conventionally dressed men in straw boaters and women in cloche hats marvelling at the exhibits.

Turin was (and still is) a handsome city of palatial eighteenth-century facades, sequences of squares, austere courtyards and arcades, set against the backdrop of the Alps on which snow is visible for much of the year. But beyond the arcades and the boulevards was proletarian Turin, the makeshift city of barrack-like blocks, quickly and badly built to house newly urbanized workers. In those days it had not yet acquired a rim of banal new apartment blocks and factories. It had not yet seen the addition of hamburgers and kebabs to the staple diet of its street cafés.

Today there is no longer quite enough life and energy to sustain its urbane qualities. Its shopfronts are shrinking back into the ever-present colonnades. A generation of artists and writers in the city has gone, and their successors have failed to emerge.

Comparing Milan and Turin, it is painfully obvious which of them has managed to make its mark as a world city, and which has not. It is enough to count the number of international departures at Linate and Malpensa, and compare them with those at Turin's airport.

Milan is not without its problems but it does have a grip on the worlds of fashion and design that any city would envy. Turin was a place where landless peasants and artisans were transformed into an urban proletariat. It was where Umberto Agnelli had set out to build a production line to make cars, inspired by what he had seen of Henry Ford's plant in Detroit. Perhaps as a direct consequence, Turin was also where Antonio Gramsci founded the Italian Communist Party. Henry Ford borrowed the meatpacking techniques of Chicago's slaughterhouses, took them to Detroit and used them to build auto-mobiles quickly and cheaply. He slung half-finished car bodies from chains like carcasses on a production line and so invented the twentieth-century factory. When American predominance in car building died, so did Detroit. In the course of a single lifetime, its elaborate opera house and its department stores and its swaggering hotels closed, and its poorer suburbs reverted to scrub.

Turin proved to be a more resilient and a more knowing city, one with deeper urban roots to draw on to ensure its survival. When the Agnellis im-ported the modern world to Turin, it had already been a city for 2,000 years. The Roman grid had left a visible mark on its fabric — under the foundations of the Palazzo Reale there are well-preserved mosaics that were once decora-tions for the floor of a sprawling Roman villa.

The Piazza Castello has a medieval brick castle keep on one side, with a baroque plaster facade attached to create the Palazzo Madama on the other. The core of Turin's urban grain is the relationship between one of its two major spaces and the other. The Piazzetta Reale and the Piazza Castello are at right angles to each other, creating what seems to be an L-shaped space. But they are interconnected, so that from the east, the two squares appear to be one much larger urban space with the Castello standing in the middle of it.

Guarino Guarini's seventeenth-century baroque masterpiece the Royal Church of San Lorenzo flanks the royal palace, yet it has no exterior presence. Instead, it is subsumed into the elevation of the square; inside there is an explo-sion of complex ambiguity, an architectural interior that reflects Turin's urban-ism, which is equally ambiguous. The roads feeding the Palazzo Reale and the Piazza Vittorio Veneto are subsumed into the colonnade systems. The facades of the great colonnaded *corsos*, are also screens that gradually reveal further courtyards, some private, others public piazzas. It's an urban pattern that finds an echo in some of the architectural drawings that Sottsass was making in the 1980s. He showed blank-walled paved squares, penetrated at each end by openings to allow streets to bisect them.

Yet Turin was also a place that was prepared to countenance violently disruptive intrusions to its fabric. Before the Lingotto, the city had already built one of the most mysterious of Europe's nineteenth-century landmarks, the Mole Antonelliana, a kind of brick-and-stone Eiffel Tower, and almost as ubiquitous in dominating so many views of the city skyline. Antonelli's monument stands as a curious memorial to the implacable determination of an architect to ignore the wishes and the resources of his clients. Soaring above the regular seven storey-high roofline of the city like a rocket, it is as conspicuous as a vertical version of the Lingotto, stood up on end. It has no particular architectural provenance, nor does it seem to belong to any particular architectural typology; it's not a palace, a cathedral, nor a parliament. The monument is named after its architect, Alessandro Antonelli, and it was originally commissioned as a synagogue by Turin's Jewish community after Italian unification in 1861. Antonelli kept revising the design to make it taller — and therefore more expensive. He proved so unbiddable that his original clients eventually abandoned the project. They swapped the incomplete monument and the site on which it stood for land elsewhere in Turin and built themselves a more plausible synagogue. The city decided to finish the project and, for a while, it was used as a museum of the Risorgimento, Italy's national struggle for unification. At the end of the twentieth century, it was converted into a museum of cinema. It was the structure that, as a boy, Sottsass could see from his home across the River Po every day, a distinctive symbol of Turin's ambitions and of the slightly mysterious undercurrents of life in the city.

For both father and son, the first year in Turin was difficult. As a twelve-year-old, half-Austrian Sottsass found himself in a new school that, as he quickly realized, he hated. He was in a class of what, to him, felt like forty schoolboy toughs, already well on the way to becoming Blackshirt street fighters. They laughed at Sottsass, with his hair so fair that it was almost white, his curious accent from the mountains and his strange name. He was bullied and he was miserable, but there were compensations to city life. 'I was fascinated and thrilled by Turin's trams,' Sottsass remembered. 'There weren't any trams in the mountains where I'd lived [...] It was great to sit in a tram and look out at the city from the window. The tram went past a square where there was a wonderful market full of colours.'

On holidays Sottsass's father would give his son the price of a ticket to go out to one end of the line and then come back again. Trams took on another significance when Sottsass began to collect those tickets. He remembered the loss of a tooth in Trento, extracted traumatically by his dentist who then told him it would never grow back. It was the moment that he realized the essential transience of things. Sottsass was already preoccupied by colour. He described his humble collection of tram tickets, arranged by colour, as an attempt to find some sort of a consolation for the loss of his tooth, and the premonition it brought of mortality.

Sottsass remembered his father as always singing when he was happy. He could hear him sing in the shower. He could hear singing from the bedroom. But there were days when things were not going well, and there were no songs.

Sottsass did the things that sons conventionally do with their fathers. He was proud of the racing bicycle that they built together:

> I made it with my father, putting together pieces from
> other bikes, and the best parts that we could find on
> the market. It was finished in black, and had no branding
> of course. The racing gears were in raw aluminium, the
> tape on the handlebars was white. Perhaps it was the first
> design that I had ever done. In silver, black and white,
> it seemed pretty elegant to me. They were the colours
> of a book my father had brought back from Vienna, that
> I had in the house as a child, *The Song of the Nibelungs*,
> illustrated in Art-Nouveau style.

The younger Sottsass's time at his first school in Turin did not end well. He failed his exams and was threatened with having to repeat a year. He spent the summer of 1930 with his mother's family in Innsbruck while his parents took stock. They were worried enough to consider going back to the Trentino to find a more sympathetic school for their son.

Sottsass remembered the day that he came home to talk to his parents about his poor results.

> My father said to me, 'Ettore, come, I have to tell you
> something.' We were in the dining room with a square table.
> There was a big plate full of coloured fruit. It was a little
> cold and the air was scented, perhaps by peaches. My
> father did not say to me, you are an idiot or something like
> that. He said to me, 'Ettore, I work hard. Life is difficult

and it is very tiring, but I am always hopeful. I have
put my faith in you. Now you too should begin to work.
Do you understand?'

In the end his parents decided to stay in Turin. Rather than repeat a year, Sottsass would receive special tuition in Latin and mathematics, and then sit the entrance exams for the Liceo Scientifico Statale Galileo Ferraris — named for one of Italy's most brilliant electrical engineers, and one of the best schools in Turin. He passed. The new school was where the city's élite sent their children, and it was where Sottsass fell in love for the first time.

At the same time his father quickly fell out with his only professional contact in the city — the engineer Galdini whose suggestion that they could work together had brought him there in the first place. His father's work was still in the Trentino, and for that he had to leave his family and travel back to the mountains every week. When he was not back in the Trentino, Sottsass senior worked at home in their apartment on the Corso Francia and kept looking for opportunities in the city. Finally, there was a chance meeting with an old acquaintance, a civil engineer named Hartunghen who steered a commission to design a cinema in Aosta toward Sottsass.

Later, when a project to build the Palazzo della Moda made Sottsass senior enough money to be able to afford to do so, he designed and built his own home and studio on via Villa della Regina. It is an impressive Modernist villa, set back from a street that climbs the green hills that overshadow this side of the city. The air is fresh, there are lots of trees and it is a refuge from the city across the river below. The house, completed in 1938, faces a retirement home that was once an almshouse, and borders a park. It would have felt detached from the city, even though it is only a twenty-minute walk to the Palazzo Reale.

The house and studio are off the main street, reached by a narrow path and a couple of flights of steps. There is still a pair of red stone pylons on granite bases defining the entrance today. Cut into one of the bases, the letter box that Sottsass's father designed for his home still survives. The two words *Casa* and *Studio* define the opposite ends of the slot, in bronze cast letters. A heavy gridded-mesh gate with rounded corners, the Art Deco font and the flourish on the lower-case 'b' hint at the involvement of a design-conscious architect.

At the foot of the hill below the house and looking back at the city is an ossuary, containing the remains of some of the unknown victims of World War I. The Sottsass family later moved into the city centre to the Piazza Vittorio

Veneto, a ten-minute stroll over the bridge that Napoleon built over the River Po from the house on the via Villa della Regina. It seems likely that Sottsass's father was forced to sell the house to support them during the war, and rented the apartment while living in the Trentino.

The piazza is a short walk along the arcades of the via Po, from the Palazzo Reale, and takes the form of a classical stadium, with a crescent at one end, colonnaded on its two long sides and open to the river at the bottom. There are shops and cafés at ground level within the arcades. The facades are finished in cream-coloured plaster. They sit on a Palladian base, a rhythmic procession of wider arches two storeys high, flanked by lower openings. They lived in an apartment at Number 9, a tenement building which today has a pair of heavy wooden doors that would have looked much the same in the 1940s. It is on the side of the piazza closer to the Mole. The Sottsass apartment had a balcony, looking out over the piazza.

In the course of ten years in Turin, Sottsass's father moved on from a series of well-crafted but essentially modest buildings to become a member of one of the most sophisticated groups of Modernists in Italy, the Movimento Italiano per l'Architettura Razionale (MIAR), even if he was overshadowed by the fame of its charismatic leader, Giuseppe Pagano. And his son had experienced enough to see a potential future very different from the one that had awaited him in the mountains.

It was a group that had more than fifty members throughout Italy. In Turin they included Gino Levi-Montalcini, Ottorino Aloisio, Umberto Cuzzi and Giuseppe Gyra as well as Sottsass senior. In essence MIAR was an attempt to make rationalism, the Italian version of Modernism, the official style of Benito Mussolini's regime. For some members it was an ideological stance, but for most it was a straightforward attempt to find more work. They worked together on large high-profile projects. They lobbied for their views to be heard and they staged group exhibitions. It was a high-risk strategy, one that in the end failed, since Mussolini always tilted towards the traditionalists.

Pagano, who as a war veteran had taken part in Gabriele D'Annunzio's seizure of Fiume in 1919, was a dedicated fascist and he joined Italy's national Fascist Party, the Partito Nazionale Fascista (PNF), very early on in its history. He was involved with the Scuola di mistica fascista, a group that attempted to create a leadership myth around Mussolini, and to devise a cultural and intellectual programme for the party. Pagano was a contributor to its journal *Dottrina Fascista*. His chief rival in the power struggle around Mussolini for

42

influence in the architectural field was Marcello Piacentini, official architect to the regime, a role that came with an elaborate gold-braid encrusted uniform and a generous salary to go with the title. Piacentini was caught between creating an intimidatingly symmetrical language for official Italian architecture that emphasized Mussolini's attempts to claim a Roman imperial inheritance and his own interest in modernity. Piacentini and Pagano co-existed, and in some cases were able to work with each other. The two designed the Italian Pavilion for the Paris Exposition of 1937 together, and succeeded in producing one of the most striking and original buildings on the site. In contrast to the massive marble and granite offerings of Germany and the Soviet Union, the Italian pavilion was a complex and subtle composition of overlapping grids that was light on the ground and inventive in its detail.

Pagano had been born an Austro-Hungarian citizen like Sottsass and his father. He grew up in Istria where Italians were a small minority, rather than in the Tyrol like Sottsass where they were more numerous. When Italy entered the war in 1915, Pagano was still a teenager. He left his home, crossed the frontier, translated his name from Pogatschnig into its Italianized version of Pagano and enlisted in the Italian army, where he was to serve with distinction.

Pagano studied at the Turin Polytechnic (as Sottsass junior would also go on to do), graduating in 1924. He was able to use his connections as an early member of the PNF to start his architectural career, designing a number of public buildings both in Milan and Turin. They had a dark, brooding and sombre quality that influenced Sottsass's father's view of architecture. And once Sottsass had opened his own office in Turin, he was to collaborate with Pagano on a number of projects.

Pagano took his version of modernity from its Austrian roots: Adolf Loos's stern rectilinear forms and Josef Hoffmann's work in such projects as the Palais Stoclet in Brussels were inspirations for him, as they were to both Sottsass junior and senior. But Pagano began his studies a decade after Sottsass senior and was driven by a much less contextual approach.

The first major project that he completed in Turin was a nine-storey-high office building for the Gualino Company, a sober exercise in unadorned architectural restraint, sometimes described as the first modern building in Italy. It takes the form of a slab-like tower, with solid walls punctuated by squat window openings, and sits on a rusticated base, topped with a stripped cornice. Riccardo Gualino founded a textile company and later became a vice president of Fiat; after the war he set up a film studio, Lux Film. Pagano designed the building to accommodate his businesses. It provided a starting point for all of MIAR's projects.

Sottsass's father was introduced to Gualino shortly after the family arrived in Turin, and had been encouraged by talk of working for him. But before the connection could come to anything, Gualino was arrested for antifascist activities and sentenced to internal exile on the island of Lipari in 1931. Sottsass senior took part in two of the defining architectural confrontations of the Mussolini years. Neither project resulted in Sottsass actually building anything. But they did push him to the centre of the architectural debate in Italy, and the attention he attracted later helped him secure several important commissions.

The first *cause célèbre* was the redevelopment of the via Roma in Turin, which the regime wanted to carry out as part of its plans to modernize Italy's big cities. Pagano and his collaborators, of whom Sottsass was one, designed a scheme for transforming the via Roma into what they claimed would be the most modern street in Europe. Their dramatic charcoal renderings show a monumental axial plan for the street lined with slab blocks punctuated by towers at intervals. Each member of the team took on the detailed architectural design of a part of the street. Their version of the via Roma would have transformed the identity of Turin in a manner reminiscent of the Karl-Marx-Allee in Berlin, creating a bold new route from the Porta Nuova station to the Palazzo Reale. Despite a great deal of initial excitement, it was too radical for the more conservative local politicians to support. Pagano and Sottsass senior were determined to fight for their project. They took their drawings to Rome and spent nine days waiting, with increasing despondency, for an audience with Mussolini that never materialized.

In the end, Piancentini got the job. He treated via Roma as a piece of complex urban surgery, cutting a triumphal route through the city. On the way from station to palace, it deftly negotiates the Piazza San Carlo with two baroque churches in the middle of its southern wing forming a choke point. By facing the backs of the two churches with granite, he created a fascist square to add to the stock of piazzas that previous generations had left behind. He used the same granite to leave a tidemark on all four sides of the Piazza Garibaldi. At the station end of the street Piacentini's colonnades assert themselves more vigorously. But at the edge of the Piazza Castello, Piacentini left the nineteenth-century facades and colonnades intact, slipping in his own designs behind them. A somewhat naïve tower, pencil thin and faced part in

44

brick, part in travertine, is a mildly shocking intrusion. Pagano left Turin for Milan shortly after the competition, where he re-established his studio, and became the editor of *Casabella*.

The disappointment of the via Roma for Sottsass senior was followed by a near-miss. It was a competition for building a new railway station on the edge of Florence's historic centre. The site was next to Santa Maria Novella, the church for which Masaccio painted his masterpiece, the *Holy Trinity*, and visible from Giotto's campanile. It could not have been a more controversial project. The design of the new station was expected both to respect one of the most sacred sites of European civilization and also to demonstrate the glories of fascism.

Plans to build a Neoclassical station on the site were abandoned after a series of violent attacks on the design by, among others, Filippo Tommaso Marinetti, founder of the Futurist movement. As might be expected from the man who had demanded that Venice fill the Grand Canal with concrete, he wanted something more expressive of his fantasies of an Italy characterized by dynamic modernity. A new competition was held in 1932, and attracted a huge amount of attention. The job eventually went to a Tuscan team, led by Giovanni Michelucci. But the jury, which included Marinetti and Piacentini, divided the second prize between Sottsass and three others — selected from 150 submissions. After all the publicity, Sottsass secured three significant commissions, suggesting that he was officially approved of, and that he was making effective use of his connections. He designed and built the Palazzo della Moda, Turin's exhibition hall for trade fairs, a seaside holiday hostel in Tuscany and a memorial to Dario Pini (a Blackshirt murdered in 1921) and what were described as fascist martyrs, killed in street fighting with communists in the Turin riots of 1922.

Italian architecture in the 1930s was going through a remarkable transformation in the turmoil of fascism. There was a chance to build a new country, or so it seemed, and Sottsass's father wanted to play a part. But to be successful it was impossible not to be a card-carrying member of the PNF. Mussolini's ramshackle ideology was ambiguous enough to accommodate almost every kind of intellectual at various points in their careers.

Marinetti with his pornographic worship of speed, violence and destruction made Mussolini look almost pragmatic. Well before the establishment of the Blackshirt gangs, he had broken into the offices of a Milanese newspaper, attacked the staff and set about destroying the presses with a crowbar. He celebrated the beauty of the roses of spreading blood created by machine guns. But there were many other Italians who were prepared to take a less brutal message from fascism.

Official commissions in the 1920s and 1930s were allocated through a system of competitions, and Sottsass senior did well enough out of it. There was his prize for Merano's town hall in 1928 worth 1,000 lire, a third prize for a school in Folgaria and another third prize for a design for a post office in the suburbs of Rome. Then came the Casa del Fascio that he built in Moncalieri in 1935 (one of a network of party buildings Mussolini put up across Italy, each with its tower and its pulpit overlooking the town square) and the 2,000 lire prize he picked up for his design for an altar sacred to the memory of fallen soldiers.

Among Sottsass's papers is the letter to his father, awarding him the prize from the PNF's Federazione dei Fasci di Combattimento of Turin. 'We want to congratulate you on the fervour and nobility demonstrated in this project which demonstrated how faithful it was to the fascist spirit. You give Turin a design suitable for its glorious traditions.' And then there was the celebrated competition for the Casa Littoria in 1938, planned for the heart of the city of the Caesars, in sight of the Colosseum, on which Sottsass worked with Umberto Cuzzi and Emilio Pifferi.

Despite their inherent qualities, these are difficult projects to come to terms with. It is not just that it was necessary for their architect to be a member of the Fascist Party to design them. The architect's designs were consciously being used by the state as a form of built propaganda.

Sottsass defended his father against the too-ready judgements of history in *Scritto di Notte*:

> Nobody today could argue that my father, like so
> many other intellectuals, writers, painters, professors,
> poets and publishers, could be labelled a fascist.
> But you cannot ignore the conditions, and the climate
> and the few possibilities available which meant that
> they found themselves in an intellectual framework
> that might be called fascist. [...] An architect, if
> they wanted to work or even if they just wanted to
> enter a competition, had to join the PNF, or to
> have a partner in some way connected with the party.
> That was the case for my father, but he didn't have
> a guilt complex about it.

Sottsass himself had to join the Gruppo Universitario Fascisti (GUF), an organization that, among other things, offered students generous discounts to the cinema and access to a student club decked with the aggressive slogans of fascism: 'Book and Musket make a good Fascist'. Members were expected to wear the GUF uniform to sit their exams, which included a preposterous comic-opera green hat and a blue neck scarf with a toggle.

It is instructive to compare the commitment of Pagano with the fatalism of Sottsass's father. Pagano had believed strongly enough in a united Italy to flee from Austro-Hungary so that he could take up arms to fight against the Empire. Sottsass may have wanted to see Trentino integrated with Italy, but he still went to war for Austria. When World War II came, Pagano volunteered to fight, then lost his faith in fascism and joined the partisans before dying in a concentration camp. Sottsass senior did what he had to, because he believed that there was no choice.

Sottsass's father was ready to respond to the prevailing climate of opinion in his approach to architecture, moving away from his emotional investment in Friedrich Ohmann's Viennese eclecticism to adopting the ruthless glamour of rationalism, and then, in the reconstruction of post-war Italy, to a more acceptable form of democratic modernity with its roots in a Mediterranean vernacular. For him, they were all equally acceptable forms of expression. None of them, it seemed, entirely represented his own view.

By 1931, when his son was fourteen, he was busy enough to be able to afford not to work from the family apartment. Sottsass was still attending the Liceo Scientifico Statale Galileo Ferraris and he was drawing all the time. He rendered wooden panels, a parallel-motion drawing board, even an ancient upright typewriter in pen and ink, with brilliant economy of means. His lines are lucid, confident and show a complete understanding of what he was looking at, not just the form of the objects, but also of how they worked and how they were made. These are drawings that already show the clarity with which he would go on seeing the material world for the rest of his life.

Some of them relate to his history lessons, such as the sketches of elaborate swagged urns and *putti*. One shows an escutcheon over a carved wooden door, on which Sottsass has inserted his own name in the heraldic shield as 'Ercole Sot Sas'. There are also drawings that show ancient fragments of tapestry, and other historical references.

It was at school, while he was making these drawings, that Sottsass gradually fell in love for the first time.

Lina [he does not mention her surname in *Scritto di Notte* but it was Musso] **went to the same school as me, but in a different class. In the afternoons, we would wander around the city, chatting, sometimes we found ourselves in the woods, in which there was a big rock, that we would sit on, looking at the lake, sitting in silence while it grew dark. Perhaps we would even kiss, maybe we held hands, and sat saying nothing because we were afraid.**

The relationship continued after Sottsass left school and started at Turin Polytechnic in 1934. In that summer, Sottsass took his silver, white and black bicycle and pedalled the 25 miles to Lina's holiday home. He climbed the 4,016 metre Gran Paradiso (one of the highest mountains in Italy) using ropes and crampons, with his uncle but no guide, and was hurt in a rock fall on the way down.

'The years passed and there were interminable walks, and then one day, like in a silent dream, we made love.' Sottsass, not for the last time, could not embark on a relationship that was both physical and emotional, without beginning to think about how it would end. 'We were aware of impermanence. One day, I knew, she was going to make love with another man, and to have a child with that man. Gradually it became clear that she did not want to be with me.' Sottsass photographed Lina several times. More than fifty years later, he published the picture that he took of her in 1937 standing on a balcony, in a striped short-sleeved blouse. Their relationship ended soon after that photograph was taken.

It was a difficult parting. Luigi Spazzapan, the painter who was an acquaintance of his father's and who became the most important influence on Sottsass in his student years, tried to talk to him about Lina, but only made him feel worse. Sottsass would see Spazzapan most afternoons, a shambling artist in his fifties, usually with a three-day growth of beard, sometimes still wearing his pyjamas in his chilly studio. Sitting on a three-legged stool at the round table in his two rooms on the eighth floor of a tenement on the Corso Giulio Cesare in suburban Turin, Sottsass remembered the air thick with the intoxicating scent of oil paint, and Spazzapan smoking cigarettes that he broke in half to share with his wife. Sottsass began talking about the love affair that was ending. 'You, Sottsass, you will make many women fall in love with you in your life,' Spazzapan told him. 'I was in love with Lina and I thought it would be forever. It was the one thing I was certain about, so when Spazzapan told me this, it was like a catastrophe for me.'

Sottsass saw Lina Musso afterwards only once. He was stepping out of a car. She was on the pavement. Sottsass suggests that she told him, 'You've really turned into a man.' In 1995, Lina's son called Sottsass to tell him that his mother was dead.

Sottsass continued to pursue what he described as his highly conventional architectural studies at the polytechnic. In fact the school had not been so conservative in its outlook as to hamper Pagano, who had studied there in the previous decade. In ascending order of complexity through his five years at the school, he designed a series of student projects that took him from 'a fountain to be built near a Roman church,' to a 'four-storey-high apartment block with balconies' and finally a town plan for an industrial city with workers' housing in parallel blocks arranged around a school, a church, a theatre, a cinema and, of course, a Casa del Fascio.

Sottsass's earliest surviving dye-line print, showing a design for a doorway, was made in 1937. He rendered his name in his capital-block typewriter script as 'Ettorino Sottsass', the diminutive version of Ettore. It was followed by an early architectural design, for a two-storey *villa per una famiglia*, under the name 'arch Sottsass Torino'. He made a measured drawing of a Thonet bentwood armchair and he designed a chapel in the form of a simple unadorned cube. But he was more interested in the time that he spent with Spazzapan in his studio, where he hoped that he could learn how to be an artist.

Luigi Spazzapan was born in 1887 and, like Sottsass, was an Austro-Hungarian citizen (in his case, of the province of Slovenia). He died in 1958 and his face is one of the images that Sottsass rendered and defaced in his memorializing lithograph at the end of the millennium. He had been in Munich at the time of the Blaue Reiter group, and in Paris when Picasso arrived. In Turin, he taught Sottsass to paint 'with the stomach and the arm, like a sort of Zen act' as Sottsass's first wife, Fernanda Pivano put it. She described Spazzapan as a proto Jackson Pollock who painted on canvases spread out on the floor. Sottsass contradicted her: 'Spazzapan didn't tell me how to paint, he showed me how to use a brush with long hair so I could do calligraphy, and how to work with a short fat brush, so that I could colour large areas.'

Sottsass was already a fluent draughtsman. But his work with Spazzapan went deeper than that. For years he struggled to understand if he should work as an artist or as an architect. Le Corbusier had the same dilemma, painting in the mornings, designing in the afternoons. Sottsass suggested: 'I was trying to explore the nomadic, elusive nature of painting. I would waste a lot of time with Spazzapan, and even more time indulging all my painting-related — specifically painting-related — curiosity, thoughts, tests, happiness and unhappiness. I might have thought I knew what architecture was. Painting, on the other hand, was a mystery, and mysteries are always more attractive.' Sottsass suggested that he looked as much at Spazzapan as a person who could show him how to live, as he did at his work.

Sottsass told a story about Spazzapan cautioning him against using yellow in the way that Matisse had used it. 'Matisse was sixty when he did that, you need many years of life to be able to paint yellow like that.' Spazzapan held court in the days before the war started in the Bar Patria, on the Piazza Castello, nursing his drinks and spending the time with a regular group of artists: Mino Rosso, Augusto Bertinaria, Giulio Da Milano and Giorgio Soavi. Sottsass was Spazzapan's closest architectural follower and Carlo Mollino would sometimes join them.

Spazzapan's rival in Turin in the late 1930s was Felice Casorati whose careful, Neoclassical and highly controlled academic work — often making explicit references to Quattrocento painters — looked to be at the opposite end of the spectrum to Spazzapan's loose expressionism. Pivano wrote in her diaries: 'In those days it was very smart to say that Spazzapan was a dauber, and it was very smart to be a follower of Felice Casorati. Casorati had a very mixed group with names like Francesco Menzio and Enrico Paolucci and a whole crowd of young followers who thought it was useful to say these things.'

From their table in the Bar Patria, Spazzapan and Sottsass could see the massive war memorial behind the castle in the middle of the piazza. It was a monolithic commemoration of the dead, rendered in the manner of the Mussolini period although without the ostentatious fascist habit of renumbering the calendar. The centrepiece was a twice lifesize Alpini officer flanking Emanuele Filiberto, Duke of Aosta. In the bar, they nursed their drinks hour after hour, and they talked about life and art.

Sottsass began exhibiting his paintings in Turin art galleries with Spazzapan and his associates in the early 1940s. Later he would write: 'These revelations, colours and the surfaces on which they are used; the switch from one colour to another, the physical qualities of colours came to me together with many others that I sought out on my own, and I have stuck to them, perhaps because they have ended up as part of my way of being an architect.'

Sottsass joined the Fascist Party in 1936 aged nineteen. His membership number was 30682. A year later, in 1937 (in fascist terms, Anno XVI) he was issued with his first passport, covered in the blue of the Italian monarchy. The photograph shows a grave young man with a moustache. He used his passport to make his first trip to Paris. (His father gave him enough money to buy a third-class train ticket.) He spent four days walking around the city, gulping down every scrap of art he could find, but said very little about the architecture. He saw colour in the works of Toulouse-Lautrec, Bonnard, Van Gogh, Gauguin, Vuillard, Vlaminck, Derain, Matisse, Braque and Léger, but it was Picasso's *Guernica*, exhibited for the first time in the Spanish Pavilion at the Paris Exposition Internationale des Arts et Techniques dans la Vie Moderne, that stunned him into silence.

This was at the height of the Spanish Civil War, and Picasso's canvas was part of the Spanish Republic's propaganda campaign against the onslaught of Franco's rebels, who were backed by Italy and Germany. The painting made a profound impression on Sottsass. What shocked him most was not the violent savagery of the iconography, but the way in which Picasso had drained colour entirely from the image. For once, Sottsass showed extreme precision in his memory of the exact size of the painting:

> I found myself in front of this rectangle 7.8 metres wide
> and 3.5 metres high, with three colours, white, black and
> a very little grey. I was paralysed. I was exploded and
> vaporized by an ambiguous space without description or
> explanation in which nature ended at an invisible horizon,
> in which there was nothing but shame and fear and ill
> feeling, humiliation and tears and screams, arms raised
> against everything. I was twenty, was this all that life had
> in store? Nothing but the brute force of beasts? When I
> recovered my power to move from this white, black and
> grey wall, I felt feverish, and I went home.

Elsewhere in the exhibition park overlooking the Seine, Sottsass saw the Soviet Pavilion, designed by Boris Iofan and topped by Vera Mukhina's representation of a worker and peasant holding a hammer and sickle, confronting Albert Speer's towering eagle-topped German Pavilion. He did not go inside: 'I knew what to expect.'

Sottsass also remembers Alvar Aalto's Finnish Pavilion and Alexander Calder's *Mercury* fountain at the Spanish Pavilion — a symbolic representation of the resistance of Spain to fascism. He went to see the Italian Pavilion, designed by his father's colleague Pagano with Piacentini, but did not discuss the design.

He stayed at Hotel Azure, near the Gare de Lyon. Sottsass described buying a light blue-and-black chequered scarf that he thought made him look very stylish and purchasing a ticket to see Maurice Chevalier sing in a cabaret. The spree left him with so little money that he had to save every penny that he could to buy exhibition tickets — so much so that he was reduced to living on bread and a can of peaches (bought under the mistaken impression that it was jam) for the three days he spent in Paris.

Sottsass declared: 'When I came back from Paris, I became a different person.' At the polytechnic he made two exam submissions under the influence of his Parisian experiences. One was for stage design, which he presented in the manner of the Cubists, the other involved furnishing an interior in the style of Matisse. He was told, he says, to resubmit in September with something more serious. If you are at a school of architecture you should not be posing as an artist.

Sottsass met Fernanda 'Nanda' Pivano in 1938, two months before his twenty-first birthday. Her family, like his, had moved relatively recently to Turin. But otherwise they had little in common. They came from the cosmopolitan port city of Genoa. Her father was the director of a bank, and was wealthy enough to run a household staffed by several servants. Her grandparents had lived in Siam (Thailand as it is now called), and she claimed that her grandfather had been the consul there. He was also, she said, involved with the establishment of the Berlitz language school. Certainly literary translation was the career that she would choose. She had a British grandparent, and had begun her education at the Swiss school in Genoa, with French and German on the curriculum right from the start.

From the first time they met, there was friction between them. It was at least in part the product of different social assumptions. While Sottsass would portray himself as the simple youth from the mountains, with a cultural leaning for the avant-garde, Pivano was from the comfortably well-off bourgeoisie. She played the piano and Sottsass, who preferred listening to records rather than to live music, asked her to stop — or so Pivano was to claim. She had been presented at the Palazzo Madama as a debutante. She was used to fine china and visiting cards. Sottsass brought her flowers that he had picked from a garden, wrapped up in newspaper and tied up with string.

Nanda Pivano's home on the via Vinzago was on the other side of the city centre from the via Villa Regina where Sottsass lived. It is part of a massive cliff of residential buildings, with heavy granite bases, stone rustication, with huge granite brackets holding up even more massive granite balconies that jut out from the brick facades, while elaborate brick cornices and pediments project further and further into space. Sottsass's father's studio house was a white-washed cube, and represented architecture reduced to its essentials.

If Sottsass was, at heart, apolitical, Pivano saw herself on the left. At her school, the Liceo Classico D'Azeglio favoured by Turin's élite, even more than Sottsass's, she had been a classmate of Primo Levi, and a pupil of Cesare Pavese, both of them highly visible, anti-fascist figures. Giulio Einaudi, who would one day become Pivano's publisher, and whose father was elected as the President of the Italian Republic in 1948, had left the school shortly before she started there. Pavese translated contemporary American writers and inspired Pivano to do the same.

In 1935, Pavese was arrested and convicted as an enemy of the state for having letters from a political prisoner in his possession. After a few months in prison he was sent into 'confino', internal exile in southern Italy. A year later Pavese returned to Turin, where he worked for Einaudi as an editor. Pavese introduced Pivano to his employer, among several other literary figures. Pavese also gave her the American edition of Edgar Lee Masters's *Spoon River Anthology*, which came out in Pivano's Italian translation in 1943.

Pivano was planning to stage Orazio Vecchi's *L'Amfiparnasso*, a piece of sixteenth-century *commedia dell'arte*, and needed a stage designer. Sottsass had been recommended to her by a friend. Sottsass's father's studio, surprisingly, had one of the few telephones in Turin in 1938 and Pivano called to invite Sottsass to her parents' home to talk about the project. The meeting, by Pivano's (not entirely reliable) account, was a disaster.

> He was very young when I met him. He had won the Littoria
> prize for stage design. He had eyes as green as a bottle
> of San Pellegrino, with the body of an athlete and the looks
> of a film star. Before he said a single word, he had shown
> me his displeasure. He had seen my bourgeois living room
> with the silk wall hangings, the mahogany piano and the

scent of white lilies. He saw my little china teacups that
my grandmother had brought back from Siam and my
white blouse. Then he asked me with heavy emphasis what
did I want with him. When he heard it was *L'Amfiparnasso*,
he said loudly, first that it was impossible to stage, second,
even if it was possible, I was clearly too stupid to produce
it successfully. And thirdly he had to go home because the
smell of the flowers was giving him a headache. Showing
him out, my bourgeois education reasserted itself, to
try to rescue this disaster of a meeting by inviting him to
a celebration; we didn't call it a party in those days, that
we were holding on the following day for my birthday,
on July 18, my 21st.

Sottsass, tells another version. He answered the telephone at his father's
studio, and Pivano introduced herself:

'Good morning, my name is Fernando Pivana, I am a
literature and philosophy graduate. I have studied the
piano for eight years, and I am now organizing concerts
for the GUF. At the conservatoire, I would like to stage
a Cinquecento opera. I have been told that you are
great at designing stage settings and I would like to know
if you might be interested.'
　　At that time I was an arrogant kid, but although
I knew little or nothing, I did know that some things were
risky and took a lot of experience. How could we find
the money, and the orchestra, when we didn't even have
a theatre? On the other hand, this lady on the telephone
had a very confident voice.
　　Her parents' house was heavy. I was almost ill in
this dark landscape of heavy wooden furniture, with
carpets and heavy curtains held back by thick cords,
with dark iron lamps. The girl, nevertheless, was calm
and smiling, with tender, vulnerable eyes and a little sad.
[Always a detail that Sottsass found irresistible] In this
dark place, she was a bright shaft of light. We talked:

'I haven't done a set for an opera before, but I could design the tickets and the posters.'

In her diaries, Pivano described Sottsass as:

...the son of a celebrated architect [Sottsass senior] who has the name of a hill in val Badia who had moved to Turin from Trento. After he had become an irredentist he was still nostalgic for his handsome Kaiserjäger uniform. He had passed on to his son an obsession with architecture and a seriousness with which he approached his work together with some highly romantic ideas, for example that he did not use a drawing board because it was a mechanical element which interfered with his creativity, and the hand's relationship with drawing.

It was, she suggested, an idea that remained with his son for the greater part of his youth, even in Milan, where for years he did not use a parallel motion drawing board, but instead used scrap paper on a wooden table.

Coming Close to the Edge

57

Ettore Sottsass joined the university officer training corps as a student. It was 1938, the year that Mussolini gave way to Nazi pressure and enacted laws discriminating against Italian Jews. Sottsass did not talk about his reasons. Perhaps he joined because he knew that it would allow him, like all of Italy's indulged university students at the time, to defer active service until he was twenty-six. He would also have his military eligibility reduced by a year. These were privileges attractive enough to double student numbers in Italian universities once Hitler had invaded in Poland.

It is the kind of inglorious expediency that his acerbic post-war scepticism would suggest. Sottsass said that he found temporary work in Fiat's drawing office after he graduated — work that might keep him out of combat. But on another level, he was following his father and grandfather who had both fought, however reluctantly, in World War I. His father had been wounded while serving as an officer in the Kaiserjäger, Imperial Austro-Hungary's mountain warfare regiment. For Sottsass to follow in such footsteps was an inevitable, even an honourable, thing to do.

The war began in fits and starts for Sottsass. He would put on his uniform for a month in one training camp or another, or for weekdays in the divisional HQ in the Turin barracks. Then he would go back to work with his father in his studio in Turin with its simple modern furniture and tranquil view over the city to the Mole.

Well into 1941, when the British were already bombing Turin, Sottsass's father was still entering architectural competitions and still building. Sottsass was writing for newspapers, painting and designing. Even as he spent more and more time in uniform, the correspondence between father and son still contained the evidence of their continuing work together. In one letter from home there was a photograph of a recently completed apartment that they had collaborated on. Sottsass was still sketching furniture layouts for his father on the way to war in Yugoslavia and sending them home in his letters. Some of the drawings, dated April and May 1942, survive. There is even a furniture layout, in the form of a set of watercolour perspectives, identified as being from

1943. It was only in the last winter of the war that there was little else to talk about but despair and fear and hunger. Sottsass did his best to comfort both himself and his anxious parents. 'There is a future,' he wrote to tell them.

War was an involuntary journey for Sottsass propelling him north into the Alps at first, then to the western front with France. He saw fighting in Bosnia, Montenegro and Serbia, then moved to Germany and back into Italy where he was stationed first on the Ligurian coast, then up in the Tuscan mountains on the Gothic line. He swerved back and forth, between boredom and terror, interrupted by fitful episodes of the superficial and unsettling semi-normality of civilian life in wartime Turin.

His posthumously published account of those years reads a little like Thackeray's picaresque novel *Barry Lyndon*, with its soldier-of-fortune hero moving from battlefield to battlefield, army to army, and lover to lover. Sottsass's book is a deadpan recital of events, some tragic, some absurd, others involving barely credible coincidences. 'I realize that I am very vague about the connections between all these stories, but in reality, I remember the things that happened to my body, and in my body, and that is it. I have gone through life like a kind of parcel.'

The experience of his years as a soldier shaped the rest of Sottsass's life. He was a witness to genocide in Bosnia, where he saw the rivers stained with the blood of Muslim women and children slaughtered by the Chetnik militia that, at the time, were the paid auxiliaries of Italy. He saw trains that had been dynamited by partisans. He experienced fear, of course, but also hunger and remorse at his lack of choices. He had lovers that he had to leave behind, and was forced to watch powerlessly as his comrades, who had escaped the partisan troops of Josip Broz Tito in Yugoslavia, were cut off without food on the wrong side of the torrential Drina river.

In Italy he saw half of his platoon wiped out by American bombers. He survived two partisan ambushes with nothing worse than a flesh wound, and emerged unhurt from a strafing raid by an RAF Spitfire that flew so low he claims to have been able to see the pilot's face.

When it was all over, Sottsass was coolly sardonic about the ridiculousness of war, and its terrible effects, not least on the fatherland that he was supposedly fighting for. He talked about the sense of shame of 'being who we were'. He talked about praying that the destruction of village houses would end, and of his desperation to stop feeling so much pity and sorrow. He would put on a brave face for his parents — '*Viva Italia*,' he signed one of his letters home — though he also expressed contempt for the *'polichetti'*, the petty political schemers of the GUF. Despite his own fear of the circumstances in which he found himself as a twenty-six year-old, he tried to reassure his parents that the war was not lost, that as a member of the Alpini Monterosa Division ('the division of iron') he would be safe and that Italy had to re-establish its honour after the surrender to the Allies and would soon be back on its feet.

Despite the evidence of his diary, the meticulous records in his notebooks, the archived photographs that he took in the Balkans, and his letters home, Sottsass was often opaque about precisely what happened to him during the war. Some of the names and the dates faded from his mind over the years. He never showed much interest in precision about such details or in consistency. In his autobiography *Scritto di Notte,* he suggests that he got to Montenegro 'more or less in 1940' when it was actually in the autumn of 1942. He talks about taking a train from Prijepolje in Serbia to Belgrade, but there was no railway in Prijepolje until the 1960s. Sottsass's literary style was elliptical. When he made a drawing, he was always precise; when he wrote, he was allusive.

The first time that Sottsass talked to me about his time in Montenegro, he described being made a prisoner of war by the Germans when Italy surrendered to the Allies. As he told it, after a period of imprisonment in Sarajevo, he was eventually released, and he set out to walk home with his men. After enduring multiple hardships (such as living in a railway tunnel for months on end and being shot at by Allied aircraft) he finally got back to Turin, to Fernanda Pivano, the woman that he would marry after the war. None of this, strictly speaking, is inaccurate, but it leaves out the details that give the story a more precise meaning.

Pivano was even more vague about the exact nature of Sottsass's war. In her diaries, published after Sottsass's death and long after their divorce, she is pitilessly frank in her account of everything about her ex-husband, except in as far as it touches on what he did between 1943 and 1945. She writes about her husband's lovers in Sarajevo, his multiple infidelities and their endless, agonizing irresolution. Despite her own anti-fascist activities, she never makes it clear that Sottsass could only make his journey home because of a decision that many Italians would have seen as dishonourable. She simply records in her diary that Sottsass came back from prison in Sarajevo an empty shell of a man. He was certainly hungry and traumatized.

Sottsass did not walk back from the Balkans, he volunteered to work for the Germans, and so qualified for a railway warrant out of Yugoslavia. It allowed him to take the train from Belgrade, stopping off for a night in Vienna. He stayed in a fleapit hotel, but claimed he was able to sell the Macedonian tobacco that he had carried in his backpack from Sarajevo. It made him enough money to walk into the Hotel Sacher to buy dinner under its crystal chandeliers. He took another train that eventually delivered him to Münsingen, the Wehrmacht training camp near Ulm. And then another that took him to leave in Turin, and then back to the war on the Italian front line against the Allied armies advancing northwards.

It was only towards the end of his life that Sottsass began to be more candid about exactly what he had done in World War II. Asked in a newspaper interview in 2004 if he had served in the army of the Repubblica Sociale Italiana (known as the Salò Republic and a satellite state of Nazi Germany), Sottsass, then aged eighty-seven, replied: 'It's a thing which perhaps I haven't explained well. But I was with that division for almost a year, although without using my weapon. Then Fernanda Pivano, my first wife, helped me to desert.'

If Sottsass had counted his training in Germany, he would have had to say that he was with the Monterosa Division for rather more than a year. He was dignified enough to refuse to look for any credit for deserting the fascist army so late in the war. 'It wasn't an heroic gesture, it was only the way to avoid being caught up in the hatred that was to follow.'

The end of the war in Italy was confused and bloody. There were at least four different groups of armed Italian fighters. On the Allied side were the remains of the Royal Army, and partisan units on both sides of the front line. On the German side was the army of the Repubblica Sociale Italiana, and an array of fascist militias of varying loyalties. Hundreds, perhaps thousands, of fascists and some Monterosa soldiers were executed even after the surrender in the chaotic months that followed. In the streets of Turin, women with shaven heads and signs around their necks identifying them as fascist spies, were hanged from the lamp posts in the Corso Polonia.

Ian Thomson's biography of Primo Levi, Fernanda Pivano's classmate before the war, recounts an episode in which two of Levi's fellow chemistry students at Turin University confronted each other in a field outside the city in the closing days of the war. Once they had been close friends, but they had now become implacable political enemies. Giorgio Cotta Morandini executed the unrepentant fascist Emilio Lagostina.

Sottsass did not suffer physical harm through reprisals against Mussolini's former soldiers, but he was subjected to what he called a silent ostracism in

Milan and in Turin. 'Fernanda's friends looked at me with suspicion. Among them only [the writer, Elio] Vittorini was good to me, so much so that he even gave me the chance to write for *Il Politecnico*.' Sottsass never forgot one angry encounter in Milan in 1946. Franca Helg, an architect, turned on Sottsass. 'You should be ashamed,' she told him, and called him 'despicable'. Sottsass didn't reply at the time. Much later he would say:

> Perhaps Helg had heard that I had been in the Monterosa
> Division. Perhaps she thought that I should have gone to
> a concentration camp instead, or that I should have fought
> and died a hero for Tito, for the glorious future of the
> communist fatherland. It didn't seem to me that there
> were many Milanese architects who took to the mountains
> to fight with the partisans. It seemed to me that most of
> the Milanese bourgeoisie moved to the Swiss border where
> there wasn't much to fight or to risk.

Sottsass was no doubt thinking of Ernesto Nathan Rogers and Vico Magistretti, who spent the last eighteen months of the war in safety in Switzerland. In fact there were at least two prominent architectural victims of German concentration camps. Giuseppe Pagano, who had worked with Sottsass's father, lost his faith in fascism once the war had started and joined the partisans. He was captured and imprisoned in Brescia, from where he led a jailbreak. After his recapture, he was killed in the Mauthausen-Gusen camp. Sottsass knew and respected Pagano. After the war ended, he and his father both joined a group dedicated to a new beginning for architecture based on what they called organic design. They named the group after Pagano. Two members of the Milanese partnership BBPR, Ludovico Belgioso and Luigi Banfi, also former fascists who turned against the regime, were jailed in Mauthausen. Belgioso survived, Banfi did not.

Sottsass's military career started with the university officer training course, drilling in a Turin barracks at weekends. Manoeuvres extended his training into autumn after he graduated in 1939. He remembered sleeping in an old mill that had been turned into a makeshift barracks on a hill by a lake, its surface mirror smooth. 'It was like a picture postcard.'

Sottsass, a man whose war was full of coincidental meetings, found that he was not the only architect in the camp. He was training alongside Bruno

Zevi, who after the war became Italy's most prominent architectural critic. The camp commander heard of Zevi and Sottsass's qualifications and those of another young architect from Naples named Silvio Radiconcini. After the war, all three of them would find themselves taking part in the establishment of Italy's association for organic architecture, an influential rebuke to the architectural legacy of fascism.

> After some days marching and pushing huge trucks and breathing in their exhaust we were ordered to report to the colonel. The colonel said that he had seen that we were architects and that he wanted us to design the stage set and the bandstand for the regimental party. We did as we were asked and the colonel was so delighted with the result that he had us all commended, even Zevi and he was Jewish.
> And in Italy, life was becoming very, very, very difficult for Jews. Zevi was under threat and was fortunate enough to escape to the USA.

The episode took place during Sottsass's earliest days in the officer training school. From September 1938 Mussolini's newly enacted racial laws theoretically excluded Jews from the army, but the inefficiency of Italian bureaucracy and the continuing power of connections meant that the laws were not always carried out.

Back in Turin, Sottsass did his best to lead life as much as he could on his own terms. He was seeing Fernanda Pivano whenever he could between end of duty and reporting back to the barracks at seven in the morning. She was already making her way as a literary translator. *Spoon River Anthology*, the American poet Edgar Lee Masters's book that she translated into Italian, was to be published in 1943. Pivano remembered getting her first copy from her publisher over lunch in a Turin café. She was eating what was presented as rabbit; she suspected that it was actually cat.

Finally Sottsass's training ended. The drilling, he said, did nothing to prepare him for the random confusion of real warfare. Sottsass was assigned to the Alpini on the basis of his proficiency as a member of the ski club that his father had helped to set up in Trento.

Sottsass was fortunate in many ways. He went to fight for his country as a beautiful young man with the lean strength of an alpine athlete and the distracted otherworldly gaze of a poet. When he finally returned from that war, he was scarred by the protracted trauma of watching his comrades die. They were killed by Yugoslav partisans, incinerated by American bombs, and shot dead by their Italian fellow countrymen as traitors. They sickened and died from typhus, and were murdered by the German troops that they had recently fought alongside. Despite it all, he still looked beautiful in 1945. He was still slender and still the same athlete who had spent his youth diving, hurdling, climbing the mountains and skiing the slopes of the Alps, and he was on the edge of a career as an artist with a remarkable understanding of the language of objects, and of colour.

In June 1940 luck briefly looked as if it was on fascist Italy's side rather than on Sottsass's. By the time that Benito Mussolini finally managed to persuade himself to declare war on the Allies, the French government had already abandoned Paris and moved to Bordeaux. France was begging for an armistice. Belgium, Poland, Norway, Denmark, Czechoslovakia and Holland were all under German occupation and the British had just barely managed to rescue their troops from the beaches of Dunkirk. This was, it seemed, Italy's chance to grab the spoils of war, without needing to spill much blood.

However, appearances were misleading. For Italy to join the war, even when it looked as if it was almost over, was still to take a massive gamble. Mussolini had to believe that Germany could finish off Britain before America and Russia became involved. Mobilizing for war was all part of Mussolini's great bluff. For twenty years he had outmanoeuvred the Italian state, its army and its king, without the resources to defeat them in a real conflict. For three years from 1940, he tried to do the same with the rest of the world.

Design was one of the most powerful weapons in Mussolini's armoury. It was the conjuring trick that created a nation that looked modern, an army that appeared powerful, and a state that seemed strong and competent, but beneath the *bella figura* surface, Mussolini's Italy was a state that had little substance.

On its own, Italy would have had difficulty confronting even an almost defeated France in 1940. To the Germans at least, it was clear that there was nothing that Mussolini could do to help to win their war, beyond not getting himself conspicuously beaten. Despite the swagger of two decades of fascism, embodied in the menacing glamour of the Duce's building programme that gave every Italian city its own intimidating Casa del Fascio and every resort a fascist holiday camp, Italy was in no position to call itself a great power. The pointless second-hand imperialism of its campaigns in Albania, Crete, Libya, Somalia and Ethiopia, had done nothing to strengthen it.

In some parts of the country, one in five adults were illiterate. Italy had half the gross national product of either Britain or Germany. Its total stock of motor vehicles in 1939 was less than 500,000 — Britain had five times as many. By most measures, Italy still needed thirty years to catch up with the level of industrialization of Britain and Germany. Retaining some grasp of reality, Mussolini hesitated for most of the first year of the war before taking his disastrous decision to attack France.

Italy's top-heavy army had yet to develop the sophisticated strategic ability needed to conduct war on several fronts. It was undermined by outdated weapons. Protected by national monopolies, Italian industry failed to develop the tanks, guns and aircraft that could match those of even such minor powers as Czechoslovakia. Italian equipment was unreliable, not just because of technical shortcomings, but also because manufacturers were ready to hide poor workmanship and substandard components by falsifying inspection records.

The Italian army did, however, have impressive uniforms. They looked glamorous, they looked Italian and they looked, somehow, modern. In 1939, the recently commissioned Lieutenant Sot-sas, as he still called himself, marched through the centre of Turin along the via Roma, with its recently completed black granite colonnade by Piacentini, in his crisp new uniform and shiny black jackboots, wearing a white shirt and a black tie, immediately behind a pair of buglers and a standard bearer. He had been chosen to command the changing of the guard at the Palazzo Reale. He wore a blue sash, carried a sabre, its blade polished to a mirror-bright finish, and marched at the head of a double file of soldiers, the honour guard accompanying the unfurled royal standard.

Sottsass was characteristically wry about the experience. 'They said that it was the custom for the King to give a gold watch to the officer in charge of the guard, who spent the night in a little room with a camp bed at the entrance to the palace. I didn't see any watches, not even one made of stainless steel. Instead a truly exceptional risotto, a real king of risottos arrived.' Nonetheless, Sottsass kept a photograph taken at the time that showed him at the head of his men, marching through the street, behind the colours.

Later, when he graduated from the officer training school, and was assigned to an élite mountain division, he wore the Cappello (the soft felt hat of the Alpini), its broad brim turned up at the back and down at the front. It had a flamboyant black raven's feather securely attached to the band. In combat he had a more modest plume screwed to the side of his steel helmet. His uniform was made from grey-green wool. There were green flames on his collar to distinguish him as an Alpini, standing out from less well-favoured divisions, and a brightly coloured woollen pompom to identify his regiment.

The Alpini were specially trained troops, a remnant of the military traditions of the vanished Kingdom of Savoy and Sardinia. Its men, recruited mainly from the high valleys of northern Italy, were organized, like British regiments, on a territorial basis. The rest of the Italian army tried to avoid the factionalism that local roots might bring.

Sottsass, as a citizen of Turin, was mobilized with the Taurinense (a name which alludes to the city's Roman name), the First Alpine Division. The Alpini were national icons. Salvatore Gotta, the novelist responsible for the words of the fascist anthem *Giovinezza*, published a children's book, *The Little Alpini*, which was read in every school in Italy. The cult of the mountains characterized by fearless skiers or bare-chested athletes climbing the peaks without maps or ropes was an essential part of Mussolini's fantasy of a muscular new Italy. Sottsass was a precise match for the description.

Sottsass graduated in 1939, and he spent the next eighteen months in Turin, interspersed by periods of military training and short-term postings to a range of barracks across northern Italy. At this stage of the war, Italy had difficulty equipping and feeding all its troops, let alone deploying them effectively. The army had more men than it knew what to do with and could countenance a less than universal call-up of its forces. For a brief period, Sottsass was a designer at the Fiat factory, working on dashboards and window handles that were seen as essential enough to the national war effort to keep him out of combat. He was still writing for the student newspaper, *Il Lambello*. His last piece was published in the issue of 25 January 1941. By this time he was using 'Ettore Sot-Sas Jr' as his byline, having written 'Ettorino Sot-Sas' until 1940, and before that, in the early part of 1937, under the pseudonym Giovanni Zeta. And he was still spending a lot of time with his artist mentor Giovanni Spazzapan.

After months of frustration at the futility of military routine in his Turin training barracks, the excitement of the crowd in Rome as Mussolini declared war from the balcony of the Palazzo Venezia baffled him. But he went to war anyway — just as his father had done in 1914.

Sottsass's father had found himself conscripted into an army for which he had no sympathy. He fought against Italy for its enemy, Austro-Hungary, even though as a lifelong Italian nationalist (albeit one with an Austrian wife and a father-in-law conscripted into the same army) he was passionately devoted to the cause of uniting his Italian speaking Austro-Hungarian province with the Italian fatherland. The younger Sottsass fought for Italy, not for fascism — a cause with which he also had not the slightest sympathy. He had seen enough of the cultural freedom enjoyed by other parts of Europe when he went to Paris for the 1937 Exposition to understand the provincialism of fascism and to reject its authoritarian nature.

Mussolini found that he could not step back from war in 1940, unlike Franco who so shrewdly managed to keep Spain neutral. His hunger for a military victory overwhelmed all other considerations. As one British officer acidly put it, Mussolini was like a man who had clambered to the top of a high diving board, and after hesitating, with last-minute second thoughts, had no option in the end but to jump. The rhetoric of the Pact of Steel with Germany and Japan, signed the previous year when Italy seized Albania, the poorest country in Europe, and his own sense of himself as the founder of fascism, left him no choice. Sottsass had no choice either. There was, even if he had wanted it, no way to escape from the war. And Sottsass, in spite of everything, was still proud of the Alpini and their mountain traditions. He sang their songs even into his old age: it was a bond that meant a lot to him.

The destruction of France by Germany gave Mussolini an irresistible and apparently risk-free target. Italy's generals were less convinced, and warned that they wouldn't be ready for a real war for at least another twelve months. Mussolini believed that if he didn't get a foothold before the French stopped fighting altogether, he would lose the chance of even a minor share of the spoils. He couldn't wait another minute for his last chance of military glory. Italy mobilized 300,000 men on its frontier with France, all the way from Ventimiglia on the coast to Mont Blanc.

The French were outnumbered, their front against the Germans to the north was collapsing, but they were still able to shrug off Mussolini's attempt at an invasion. The French fleet shelled Italian fuel dumps in Genoa. The RAF bombed factories in Turin and attacked Italian supply lines. Mussolini marched his men to the top of the hill, and then he marched them down again. The war with France ended inconclusively after two weeks, at the cost of almost 700 Italian and 150 French lives. Mussolini — who had told his army commander Pietro Badoglio, 'I need only a few thousand dead so that I can sit at the peace conference as a man who has fought' — was humiliated by the campaign despite his bluster. The Allied air attack on Turin reduced him to telegramming Hitler for help. Mussolini wanted to swap an Italian armoured division for German anti-aircraft guns, crews and ammunition, an offer that Hitler did not take up.

No sooner had the armistice between France and Italy been signed, than Mussolini demobilized half his men so that the conscripts could go back home to their villages to bring in the harvest. Many were chaotically remobilized three months later in an incompetent attempt to invade Greece. Throughout this period, Sottsass was in Turin, well away from the fighting, based in the barracks through which thousands of young conscripts passed to be issued with their uniforms, their equipment and their personal weapons. At the end of 1940 he was sent to the val Formazza on the Swiss border to train Alpini soldiers from the independent ski troop of the sixth Regiment of Alpini Artillery. He was there for three months, billeted in a mountain inn. Every day he and his men would cover between ten and fifteen kilometres on what Sottsass described as a beautiful piste. In the early part of the following year, he was dispatched to an artillery training battalion until the summer of 1941. This was Alpine territory that he knew well from his youth. 'I was at Fenils on Sunday. Do you remember that little pass at Cesana da Ulzio that was on the right? What a mountain! My God, what isolation,' he wrote to his father.

It was only in February of 1942 that Sottsass finally got called up for full-time active service. He wrote to his parents regularly, sometimes two or three times a week, throughout the war. The beginning of his overseas war is marked by a letter to them with sketches of his boots, his water bottle and the eagle insignia that he asked them to buy for him to put on his Cappello.

His unit was bound for Greece. In the second week of March, on the way south by train from Turin to Bari where he was to board a troopship, Sottsass became ill. He reported unbearable pain in his ears and was hospitalized with a fever. The diagnosis was otitis media, an infection of the inner ear. It is a severe and debilitating condition. The army doctor in Bari told him that he was not fit to go to war. While his unit sailed, Sottsass remained in hospital, then went back to Turin on extended sick leave.

Even in the midst of a world war, Italy was reluctant to abandon a distinctly unmartial and unhurried routine. Officials at the war ministry in Rome went home at 2pm each afternoon. Sottsass was required to report to the barracks during his sick leave, but he was still able to return to his mentor Spazzapan, where he continued to develop his painting skills.

Emerging from Spazzapan's studio on one visit, he encountered his army doctor. 'He looked me in the face, smiled and extended my leave. Perhaps he understood that I was anything but a soldier.' Then Sottsass was ordered to report to an Alpini regiment based in Rho on the same day that he had planned to open an exhibition of his drawings in Turin. He didn't think a day more or less was going to make much of a difference, so it was only on the day after the opening that he set off on a stopping train from Turin. A girl and a man who seemed very old, but was in fact only fifty, got on at a darkened station in the middle of nowhere and sat down in Sottsass's compartment. Sottsass, preoccupied with the prospect of going to war, found himself in conversation with the girl and ended up talking about architecture. 'Suddenly, the man said, "You are Sottsass." I also had a flash, "And you are Gio Ponti."'

It was another of the random coincidences that marked Sottsass's life. Ponti had recently left *Domus*, the magazine that had become the most influential voice on Italian architecture and design since he established it in 1928. He had fallen out with the publisher, and set up a rival magazine, *Stile*.

Sottsass had published a piece in *Il Lambello* that he later remembered as an attack on Ponti's work, comparing him unfavourably with Le Corbusier. It reads as an entirely innocuous summary of contemporary developments. Sottsass was charmed by Ponti, but, in what looks a little like self-dramatization, later claimed to be mortified by what he had written, and said that he tried to apologize. He also recalled that Ponti graciously told him there was no need.

Sottsass got off the train at Rho, and went in search of the Alpini's local headquarters. He found that the regiment had already left. It was only then that he learned that the Alpini had been deployed to the Soviet Union, part of the three divisions that Mussolini sent to the Eastern Front to avoid being sidelined as he had been in France.

The account in Sottsass's autobiography is inconsistent. At one point he suggests that he was joining his regiment in Chivasso, rather than Rho. It also seems more likely that Sottsass encountered Ponti on a train at some point, rather than the same train that was taking him to the Alpini on the day that he missed going to the Eastern Front.

Sottsass often talked about the nature of luck, and the part that it played in keeping him alive. He whimsically suggested that meeting Ponti on that train was what brought him the good fortune that kept him alive during the war. He described Ponti as a kind of mascot or guardian angel. Certainly after the war was over, and Ponti had returned to the editorship of *Domus,* he supported Sottsass by publishing his work. At another point he suggests that his luck was a mysterious shrouded figure. Sottsass had certainly been extraordinarily lucky to miss that troop train to Russia. It would have taken him to the twentieth century's version of the hell depicted by Pieter Bruegel the Elder in his *Triumph of Death.* One Italian survivor of the Eastern Front, like Sottsass a lieutenant in an Alpini division who did go to Russia in 1942, recorded an almost unimaginable catalogue of horrors from wholesale slaughter to cannibalism, and spirit-crushing prison camps run by Stalin's secret police.

Of the 45,000 officers and men who left Italy for Russia, fewer than 6,000 came back alive. The rest were wiped out by two years of continuous warfare, disease and hunger. Survivors, such as the Rationalist architect Giuseppe Terragni, returned broken by what they had endured. There is a memorial to the Italians who died in Russia on the facade of Guarini's church in Turin. They died fighting for their country it says. On the other side of the square is another aesthetically more ambitious monument to the Italian victims of the concentration camps sent there by the same dictator who dispatched the army to the Soviet Union.

Sottsass was not unscathed by the war. He suffered bullet wounds. He was horrified at the sight of Bosnian women and children being massacred by the murderous Chetnik militia that were supposedly his allies. He was threatened with summary execution in a prison yard by the Ustaša (the much more savage Croat version of the Blackshirts). In the last six months of war, as Italy collapsed into anarchic chaos, Sottsass had gone hungry. Yet he was lucky all the same. His war could so easily have been so much worse. At least three times he came dizzyingly close to the edge, to being propelled from danger into horror. And each time, he survived.

There was nothing more than his luck to protect him from the random interaction of military railway timetables and the progress of the paperwork for an application for home leave. It was luck that made Sottsass start his journey home on leave from Yugoslavia on the very day that Italy surrendered to the Allies. If he had been scheduled to travel on a different train, on a different day, he would have been with the rest of the men of his division on the day of the Italian surrender. They were interned by the Germans and sent to labour camps where many were killed or starved, and survivors later fought with the partisans. Sottsass wasn't with them. It took more than a month of prison, followed by five months in a labour battalion, but in the end he returned home.

It is a sequence of accidents that may have given Sottsass his almost whimsical view of the futility of ambition, a view that was eventually to propel him into the direction of Hindu-inspired fatalism.

After missing the transport to Russia, Sottsass took a train back to Turin to the divisional headquarters to see his commanding officer. He was relieved to avoid the court martial for being absent without leave that he had half expected. As Sottsass records it, he was taken to his commander, who asked him to explain himself: '"Sir, yesterday, I went to Rho to join the regiment, but they weren't there, they had left for Russia." The colonel was furious. "What, those pricks left for Russia, and didn't let me know?" There was a burst of telephone calls, and then when he calmed down, he asked me, "And you, Sottsass, what are we going to do with you, shall we send you after them, or are you going to stay here?"' Sottsass claims to have replied that perhaps it would be better for him to stay.

In August 1942 he was sent not to the Ukraine but to the safer posting of Fort du Mont Chaberton, 3,000 metres up on the frontier with what was by now the Italian administered zone of Vichy France. This was where Mussolini's attack on France of June 1940 had come to a humiliating standstill. Chaberton was one of the chain of artillery forts on the Alpine Wall built by Italy in the 1930s to threaten each its neighbours: Yugoslavia and Austria in the east, and Switzerland in the north as well as France. (They were also an insurance against Hitler.) Substantial parts of these extraordinary structures grafted on to vertiginous eruptions of bare rock, looking remarkably like the Futurist architectural fantasies of Antonio Sant'Elia, still survive. Within hours of Mussolini's declaration of war, French garrisons in their own Alpine forts confronting the Italians had succeeded in disabling six of the eight huge guns on massive concrete turrets of Fort Chaberton with artillery fire at a range of several kilometres.

Sottsass's men were ordered to hold the fort after the damage had been done, though there was no longer an enemy to confront. The Alpini built a timber stockade within its shattered concrete walls and sat down to wait to be sent somewhere more dangerous.

Sottsass could see the green French valley far below. He looked down at the tiny houses dotted in the fields with smoke rising from their chimneys. In the evenings a couple of his men would often go down the Italian side of the mountain and return with sacks of potatoes scavenged from the fields. Sottsass spent much of his time up in the clear light of the mountains, watching circling birds of prey and using his fixed focus box camera to photograph the ruins of the fort and its broken guns.

The War

73

After missing the war both in Greece and the Soviet Union, the late summer of 1942 saw Lieutenant Sottsass and his men sprawled across the ground at the railway station in Mestre, waiting for a troop train to take them to Yugoslavia. Italy's war in the Balkans was not going well. Mussolini was sending more soldiers in an effort to rescue a difficult situation. Sottsass and his battalion were resting on their packs. He remembered the men beginning to sing one of the songs of the mountain communities from which most came: 'On the 24th of July when the corn is ripe, if you are hungry look far away.'

'It started with a single voice, loud and clear. The rest listened in silence. Then a couple more began to sing with him, then twenty then fifty,' Sottsass among them. It was, 'a long, slow, dark chorus.'

Sottsass and his Alpini were part of a fresh batch of troops sent to reinforce the Italian Second Army as it prepared for 'Operation Trio', a combined attack on Yugoslav partisans by the Italians, the Germans and the Croat Ustaša forces intended to ensure that there could be no local support for any Allied landing on the Adriatic coast.

The Alpini went by train to Mostar, the Bosnian town by that time swarming with almost 30,000 Italian soldiers, more than a third of its peacetime population. The Taurinense took over the positions left by the Pusteria Division as they moved into action to the north and east to confront the partisans.

Sottsass's unit followed the fighting, and moved through a number of villages that had already been cleared of partisans, including Foča where Josip Broz Tito, the partisan leader, agent of the Comintern and future president of Yugoslavia had based his headquarters.

Sottsass arrived in Yugoslavia at one of the bloodiest periods in the long and tortuous history of the Balkans. Hitler had cultivated Belgrade before the war to the extent of supplying Yugoslavia with modern aircraft and weapons. However, just as the country was about to sign a formal alliance with Germany, the pro-Axis government was overthrown by a group of Serbian officers. Hitler was furious and ordered an invasion to punish them. His onslaught involved assembling armies from four different countries with impressive speed. The war began with a massive bombing raid on Belgrade. By some accounts it killed as many as 5,000 people. The bombing was the prelude to an invasion by German, Hungarian, Bulgarian and Italian ground troops. The Yugoslav army surrendered in less than a fortnight.

This was only the beginning of an ever more brutal and confused war. The country, established in a burst of pan-Slav idealism by the Versailles conference in the aftermath of World War I, imploded. Three years of horror followed.

Whilst they were divided between the Austro-Hungarian and the Ottoman empires, the Balkans had experienced three centuries of relative stability. Most of the many ethnic and religious groups in the area could be found on either side of the Imperial frontier, and were able to coexist and adapt to very different political systems. The Ottoman rulers of Bosnia used their Christian subjects as tax fodder, and confiscated their children for the civil service in Istanbul, but Orthodox Christians, Catholics, Muslims and Jews lived in the same towns and villages peacefully enough for most of the time. Austria invested in roads and railways, and tax collectors to pay for them. They maintained a functioning civil service and legal system.

The simultaneous collapse of Austro-Hungary and Ottoman Turkey, and the establishment of the Kingdom of Yugoslavia transformed the ethnic and religious landscape. What had been majorities became minorities in the land that they had occupied for generations. Minorities in some provinces became the majority within a new national entity.

Provincial boundaries in Yugoslavia were extraordinarily contentious and were manipulated by each community in their attempts to turn minorities into majorities. After the maps were redrawn, and the balance of peoples still wasn't to the taste of some, the monstrous idea of ethnic cleansing was born. If the maps didn't coincide with sectarian ambitions, murder could do the job instead.

Within the new frontiers of Yugoslavia, the broken traces of the past were still glaringly obvious. The coast north of Montenegro to the Italian border, and inland around the capital Zagreb, was the Croatian heartland. It was an area with a narrow majority of Catholics — which is to say a majority of Croats — but also occupied by large numbers of Orthodox Christian Serbs, Muslims, some Roma, Jews and Albanians.

Croatian nationalist ideologues regarded the Muslims as an ethnic Croat élite who had converted to the religion of their Ottoman overlords 500 years earlier, and thus were an essential part of the new Croat nation. By claiming them as their own, rather than Serbs, or a distinct Muslim entity, the Croats would be the overwhelming majority in Croatia. Moving inland into Bosnia, the proportion of Muslims and Serbs increased as the Croats decreased in numbers. The Serbs in Croatia and Bosnia looked to Serbia, not so far to the east, and to their close cousins in Montenegro, to the south, for support.

In the two decades since the establishment of the Kingdom of the Serbs, Croats and Slovenes, commonly known as Yugoslavia, by the treaty of Versailles, the mix had proved violently unstable. In 1928 five Croat deputies were shot in the debating chamber of the Belgrade parliament by a Montenegrin member; three died at once, and the others were badly wounded. A Macedonian agent working for the Croats murdered the Yugoslav King Alexander I in Marseilles in revenge. Mussolini provided training camps for the Croat exile Ante Pavelić's fascist militia, the Ustaša.

Even before Yugoslavia had surrendered, the Axis attack provoked the Croats to declare their own state. Germany and Italy divided the rest between them. The Croatian coastal zone and Montenegro were Italian controlled, while Serbia and inland Bosnia were German administered.

Germany was fighting in Yugoslavia for strategic reasons: it needed to protect its oil supplies in Romania. The Italians had territorial ambitions for the coast. They annexed Kotor, Dubrovnik, Sibenik and Split, once Venetian cities, which immediately brought them into conflict with their supposed Croatian allies and with the Montenegrins.

The Croat Fascist Party established concentration camps, and its Ustaša militia set about slaughtering Serbs with a savagery that dismayed the Italians, and even the Germans. Curzio Malaparte, the Italian fascist turned Stalinist then Maoist writer, and Adalberto Libera's troublesome client for the Casa Malaparte in Capri, published a hideous and clearly fictional account of an encounter in which he suggested that Ante Pavelić, the Croat dictator he was interviewing, had a basket beneath his desk, full to the brim of jelly-like matter. It looked as if it were made up of oysters but Malaparte suggested that it was actually a collection of the eyes of slaughtered Serbs sent to him by his faithful Ustaša.

Since they didn't have the manpower to control the Balkans, the Germans tried to use the Croats to stabilize the country. Genocidal brutality by the Ustaša was doing the opposite. It had the effect of driving more Serbs into taking up arms against the occupation forces.

The remnants of the Yugoslav army dominated by Serb officers spawned another militia, the Chetniks. At first they fought the Germans, although by the time that Sottsass arrived in Yugoslavia they had been driven out of Serbia and into Montenegro and Bosnia where some at least began to behave as brutally to the Muslims as the Ustaša were treating the Serbs. Just as the Croats wanted to kill enough Serbs to create an ethnic majority in Croatia, so the Chetnik Serbs tried to kill enough Muslims to form an overwhelming Serb majority in Bosnia.

Yugoslavia's Communist party also took up arms. Its partisan units were the only force committed to maintaining the Yugoslav state as a single national entity. In the first few months after the invasion, the communists fought alongside the Chetniks, but the alliance quickly came apart. The partisans alienated the Montenegrins by mass executions of what they claimed were their class enemies. From this mess, the partisans emerged as politically the most adroit faction. Tito gave Milovan Djilas, his ablest lieutenant, the task of building an ethnic coalition in Montenegro. The Germans and the Italians recognized the partisans as their most effective enemies. It took longer for the Allies to do the same.

The Italians had begun recruiting and arming the Chetniks to defeat the partisans on their behalf. It was a strategy that made Sottsass's war an easier one for a while. In *Scritto di Notte*, Sottsass went further in acknowledging the details of what happened to him in the course of World War II than he was ready to do in public while he was alive. It wasn't written as a self-serving piece of exculpation. Instead it leaves clues that seem to answer charges that are nowhere precisely spelled out. Nevertheless it provides an alibi that clears Sottsass of having been at the scene of one of the worst of Italy's wartime atrocities in Montenegro.

Sottsass never hid the fact that he had been stationed in Pljevlja, but in *Scritto di Notte* he takes care to explain not only that he was there but also when and in exactly which unit: an engineering battalion of the Taurinense.

This is significant because when Sottsass and his men arrived in the town late in 1942, they had not been the first Alpini to pass through that year. They had been preceded to Pljevlja by the Pusteria Division. Sottsass records how its officers were billeted in houses around the town, and how on the night of 1 May 1942 partisans went from house to house, killing any Italian that they could find. The Italian commander in Yugoslavia, Alessandro Pirzio Biroli, had previously threatened punishment shootings. The front page of the occupier's weekly newspaper *Notiziario di Pljevlja* carried a notice in January 1942 — curiously written only in Italian — announcing that the military governor had decreed that fifty civilians would be shot dead for every Italian officer killed. For every private soldier it would be twenty civilians. The Germans had already announced their own more democratic tariff. For every one of their men killed one hundred civilians would be slaughtered.

Kurt Waldheim (who was to become United Nations General Secretary and President of Austria) was the German liaison officer with the Italians when they were attacked in Pljevlja. He was there three days later, on 4 May 1942, when seventy-four hostages were shot and hundreds of civilians were deported. It was certainly a war crime, and after 1945, the Yugoslavs tried to send those responsible to trial, but the Allies refused to countenance any war trials of Italians. In any case Sottsass was blameless, safe in Turin on sick leave, working on his drawing board when the shootings took place, and had as yet not set foot in Yugoslavia.

For years Waldheim claimed that he had never been to Montenegro. When he finally admitted that he was once stationed there, he said that he had not seen any partisans in the weeks that he was in Pljevlja. All he did was drink tea with the Italian commander and give chocolate to the local children, he said. It was the revelation of this episode forty years later that led to Waldheim being accused of war crimes, and contributed to the US declaring him *persona non grata* in 1987, after he had been elected Austrian president.

The Pusteria Division was repatriated after the massacre, and replaced in August by the Taurinense advance party. Sottsass does not mention either Waldheim or the hostage shootings in his account, though he did describe the partisan attack on the Italians. He did not arrive in Pljevlja, he said, until after the other Italians had left, though without saying why it was so important to labour the point.

Sottsass's parents stayed in Turin until September 1942. It was from there that they sent Sottsass his first letter during wartime. Their address was printed right across the back of the envelope in a bold, stylish serif face. Military post sent to soldiers stationed in Italy had conventional addresses. Sottsass's mail when he was in Montenegro was sent to him at *1 Btg Per DA Taurinense 121 Artieri Posta Militare 200*. Among the many striking things about the wartime correspondence between Sottsass and his parents is the degree to which father and son adopt the same handwriting, flamboyantly zigzagging across the page mirroring each other. Shortly after the letter was posted, Sottsass's parents moved to the comparative safety of the Trentino. They spent most of the rest of the war in Pozza di Fassa.

Sottsass's letters were often only obliquely about the war, and not because of the military censors who seem to have been remarkably ineffectual.

The efficiency, or lack of it, with which the Italian army looked after its officers is laid bare by what he had to say in his letter of 23 July 1943. He wrote to thank his parents for the parcel that he had received from them. It contained soap, a shaving mirror, four vests, seven shirts with short sleeves, three long-sleeved in wool, and three in flannel, a towel, and three pairs of socks — the basics that Italian quartermasters could not provide. Four days later he wrote saying he was sick with diarrhoea that was getting him up ten times a night. He blamed it on drinking water from a river in which he later discovered the corpse of a dead horse.

Pljevlja was a strategically important town at the intersection of Montenegro, Bosnia and Serbia, 60 miles from Sarajevo, and 100 miles inland from the Montenegrin coast. Having beaten off the partisan attack, the Italians, the Chetniks they armed, the Germans and their Ustaša auxiliaries drove them out of Montenegro. These same Chetniks then set about slaughtering Muslims in the villages around Pljevlja. The Chetnik leadership recorded the burning of at least 200 settlements, and probably slaughtered 10,000 Muslim villagers. This genocide was scarring the hills around the town. However, from the time that Sottsass arrived until the Italian surrender to the Allies in September 1943, Pljevlja itself was relatively quiet. The Italians held the towns and the Chetniks controlled the countryside. The Chetniks and the partisans were fighting it out in the mountains for most of Sottsass's year in Yugoslavia, but in Pljevlja itself, there were days when the war could be almost forgotten. Sottsass remembers a diving competition between the Italians and youths from the town, jumping from Pljevlja's bridge into the River Tara. Sottsass had excelled at diving since his childhood, and put up an impressive display. Afterwards, a local girl came to speak to him. Her name was Leonora; she was a Serb.

'I told her that it was not easy for an Italian officer to be seen talking to a Serb girl on the pavement. Maybe it was more difficult for her than it was for me.' But they met again more privately anyway. Leonora was a communist, the daughter of a well-to-do family and a medical student home from Belgrade University. She gave Sottsass his first insight into the complex nature of the conflict that he was unwittingly caught in the middle of. What, she wanted to know, were the Italians doing as allies of the Germans?

Sottsass's unit comprised eight men and a sergeant. They had a truck and a heavy machine gun that Sottsass claimed was never fired in combat. Their job was to keep the roads and bridges open all the way to the divisional headquarters in Nikšić, fifty miles southwest in the centre of Montenegro. The hills, which they patrolled in the late summer of 1942, had a pellucid beauty that made the horrors that were taking place in them all the more shocking.

'It was strange in all this sharp, clear light, in this cosmic silence, to find on the ground in some dark wood, a corpse, its mouth open, with ants crawling in and out. Perhaps he was a Muslim man killed with some invisible knife, or a Croat man killed by a shot from who knows where, or an exhausted partisan, killed by fear, by tiredness, by hunger.'

Throughout his time in Yugoslavia Sottsass had a camera with him. In the early days of the war, it was a simple box camera — later, he was able to afford a Leica. His photographs record a strange adventure, moving from images of the impeccably turned-out Italian troops in holiday mood as they went to war and ventured into the hinterland of Montenegro, where his camera lingered over the needlework, lacemaking and weaving of peasant women, to suddenly reveal railway locomotives upturned and broken across the tracks as the Italians found themselves in the midst of one of Europe's most brutal and vicious guerrilla wars.

The photographs that he took in the hills above Pljevlja during the snowy winter of 1942 show Alpine landscapes that looked a lot like the Trentino in which he had grown up. An old farmer in a cloth cap and a long black overcoat picks his way through the snow under the gaze of an Italian soldier, rifle slung over his shoulder. A couple of Alpini in their folkloric hats and capes march through the fields. A patrol of Italian soldiers in the distinctive steel helmets of the period, a modernized version of Imperial Roman headgear, carrying an assortment of weapons across their shoulders, winds its way single file down the slope of a hillside. The photographs show peasant women in their intricately embroidered costumes, waistcoat over white blouse, ankle-length skirt, and white headscarf hiding their hair. They show his platoon, posing in front of a great concrete bridge over the River Tara which Sottsass incorrectly believed was designed by Robert Maillart. Shortly after the picture was taken it was destroyed by the partisans with the help of the engineer that built it. The Italian soldiers are clustered around a Chetnik militiaman dressed in a black uniform.

In Sottsass's archive at the University of Parma, there are other drawings made around the same time. When he had no paint left, he drew the patterns that he saw as black ink outlines and annotated each of them, precisely describing each colour with carefully chosen words. He wrote to his parents begging them to send him more paints and more coloured inks. He was sometimes hungry, but he could not live without colour.

As the harsh mountain winter set in, the green hillsides disappeared under the snow. When the Italians went on patrols, outside the limits of the town, they could be caught in skirmishes that saw them fighting for days at a time but little was said about it in the barracks. Once Sottsass was sent to guard a remote crossroads by an old Austrian fort in the mountains.

> The landscape was white and we were sheltering in the big, empty frozen rooms of the fort, with empty windows. We made a lot of smoke with our fire, but not much heat. One afternoon six Chetniks and their leader appeared. They were dressed all in black with bandoliers, and armed with long rifles, looking like they were in a Pancho Villa movie. In vague German, the leader explained to me that in the woods was the body of a Serb, killed by Muslims. He talked about the friendship of Chetniks and Italians. He wanted us to come and see for ourselves, and report back to our commander. I felt as if I was charged with the honour of Italy.

Sottsass took half his platoon with him, leaving the truck and the machine gun, and set off to see what had happened. Only after Sottsass had left the fort did it occur to him that it was the machine gun that the Chetniks were really interested in and that they might be prepared to kill his men to seize it. It was too late to worry. The Chetniks took him to their village where they offered a meal, served by women dressed all in black just like the men. Italians and Chetniks both got drunk on slivovitz around the fire.

Sottsass duly set off, saw the body with horror and returned to the Austrian fort and the rest of the patrol. They had been anxiously awaiting his return. 'The major had been calling me to report back to him for the past two days. Fear of him made me carry out my only heroic act in all my time in the army; I skied back thirty kilometres to surprise the major and make my report.'

It was only when the partisans finally pushed the Chetniks out of eastern Bosnia that the Italian positions were directly threatened, and the Germans were drawn into the conflict. By the spring of 1943, Italy was strategically paralysed. The Allies had landed in Sicily, and were ready to invade the mainland, a move that would lead to the arrest of Mussolini by the king and Italy's surrender within a few months.

Sottsass of course knew nothing of this, but it shaped his daily existence. The General Staff had no policy to give the army and there were no larger objectives for his division. His unit did no more than do its best to stay alive.

Pljevlja was a town of 20,000 people that stood on the old caravan route from Istanbul to Dubrovnik, passing through Sarajevo. For Sottsass, still only twenty-five, it was a place to look for emotional as well as physical refuge.

There had been a Roman city not far away, and there was a medieval monastery on the edge of town, a relic of the Serbian kingdom that had been overwhelmed by the Ottomans a century before they took Constantinople. Sottsass's photographs show Pljevlja's greatest landmark, the mosque, completed around 1569, with a square stone clock tower rising over the town, alongside a needle-thin minaret which at forty-two metres had been one of the tallest in the whole of what was once Yugoslavia. The minaret and the clock tower survive today.

The mosque was built by Husein-Paša Boljanić, a Bosnian-born vizier who prospered in the service of the Ottoman court. The vizier had been a colonial governor in Egypt and Iraq before returning home and creating a monument for the town that could reflect the importance he wanted it to acquire. As custom dictated there was a fountain, a bazaar and a hammam to go with the mosque. At the height of Istanbul's power the town prospered. As the Ottoman state declined, so too did Pljevlja. Concerned at the instability that a vacuum in the Turkish provinces neighbouring its border would bring, the Austrians used the Treaty of Berlin to extract the right to station troops in Pljevlja and Sarajevo. They built the barracks and the hospital that Sottsass and his unit commandeered.

In addition to the Grand Mosque, Pljevlja had three other smaller mosques. Sottsass explored them all, along with the surviving timber houses built by the Muslims. Many had gone, destroyed if not by war then by the two serious fires that swept through the town in the nineteenth century. The Serbs lived in simple stone houses that were not so different from what Sottsass could have seen in Italy on the other side of the Adriatic. The elaborate wooden houses of the Muslims were different: they fascinated Sottsass, just as they had fascinated Le Corbusier on his journey through the Balkans before World War I. Sottsass photographed the mosques, the fountains, the graveyards and the houses. He photographed the women that he met and the carpets that they wove and left hanging on lines outside their front doors to beat out the dust. He wrote an essay on the qualities of the architectural vernacular. His fascination for Montenegro was in sharp contrast to the official ideology of the occupying Italian army, which represented the Slavs as its racial inferiors. His interest in the vernacular architecture of the area is an echo of the exhibition on rural Italian architecture organized by Giuseppe Pagano with Guarniero Daniel at the Milan Triennale in 1936. Sottsass had seen the exhibition, and been much influenced by it. When the war was finally over, and Italy could start its reconstruction, there were elements of the simplicity and directness of this architecture without architects that would guide Sottsass's own work.

In the midst of the bloodshed all around him, Sottsass came to see one house in particular as a kind of refuge. It was there that he met a young Muslim woman that he called only 'Geka'. She lived in one of the little two-storey wooden houses around Pljevlja with her widowed mother. She was, Sottsass remembered:

> a little big, a little round, with a pretty, peasant face. I wasn't in love with her but I was happy to be with her on the floor, all wood and warm. I thought I had found a home in the midst of all the chaos of war.
>
> Her ancient mother was thin and dressed in loose soft cloth, which seemed beautiful to me. She dressed like the women of Algiers as painted by Delacroix and she smoked white cigarettes. From her lips came a spiral of smoke. Geka was also dressed in wide Turkish trousers with a short waistcoat above a shirt open over her ample breasts. She was sitting at a loom, she made bags, little carpets and cushions from coarse, brightly coloured wool [...] after a while I managed to get her to weave a few rugs and cushion covers that I had designed. She was surrounded by baskets stuffed with balls of wool in every colour. At that point I was already starting to pursue the colour dimension. I thought I had to do something with all the colours around me. I was very excited.
>
> I didn't know a word of Serbian, she knew a few words of Italian, maybe she learned them to make love with some Italian soldier.

He recalls being hypnotized by her dark hair and eyes, and, one night, had sex with her.

In Montenegro that winter, death did not come only from bombs and bullets. There was also a typhus epidemic to be faced. Sottsass's diary notes that typhus killed seven out of ten of those who contracted it, and that the Italian army doctors had no medicines against it. In his barrack room some time after his night with Geka, Sottsass found a louse on his pillow. Given that lice are typhus carriers, Sottsass regarded the presence of an insect in his bed as amounting to a death sentence. Geka told him that her brother had been ill with the disease. Sottsass assumed that he had caught typhus while he was in her house. Terrified, he asked for leave to go home to Italy.

His commanding officer signed the papers, and he was able to take a series of trains to get home by way of Belgrade, Zagreb and Ljubljana. Troops returning to Italy during the war from overseas were obliged to spend a fortnight in quarantine. Sottsass found himself at the beginning of 1943 in a hotel in Grado, just by the frontier. His clothes were taken from him to be boiled and sterilized while he was deloused. He was pronounced clear of the disease, but was horrified to discover that at least one louse had survived and was still crawling over his skin. He spent the rest of the time waiting to go home, drinking himself into insensibility with glass after glass of grappa with his fellow officers.

When Sottsass got back to Pljevlja, the war had come closer. A young officer that he had become friendly with on the train on the way to Grado, had come back from leave earlier than Sottsass and been killed in a night ambush. Tito had succeeded in pushing the Chetniks back and without their shield the Italians were retreating. After the snow thawed, Sottsass and his men were withdrawn to divisional headquarters in Nikšić, while the Germans went on the offensive against both the partisans and the Chetniks. Leonora the Serb came with him on the move. She wanted to see her family in Nikšić and Sottsass gave her a seat behind him in the truck. Sottsass claims that he had little to do when they got there. In the mornings his role was supplying the officers' mess with food from the market, and in the afternoons he saw Leonora.

In September of 1943, Sottsass successfully asked his major for more home leave. He wanted to see Fernanda and his parents. He wanted to be there in time to celebrate his twenty-sixth birthday. Before leaving, he went back to Pljevlja, to take Leonora home and to say goodbye to Geka. It was a difficult parting. As Geka held him in her arms, she whispered that she had missed a period. 'Perhaps if I go and sit in the running water of the river it will come.'

The following morning, 7 September, he went to say goodbye to Leonora. They kissed for the last time, and he set off for Italy and his leave. He telegrammed his parents to let them know that he would be home in time for his birthday. 'I will probably be in Trieste on the 12th, certainly by the 14th.' But he wasn't to reach Italy for another six months.

Sottsass spent his last day as a junior officer in the army of the Kingdom of Italy, which was about to cease to exist, on a crowded troop train winding its way through the mountains of Bosnia. He was on the way to Belgrade to catch the train that would take him home. Starting the journey on that particular day was another of the many random coincidences that marked the turning points in Sottsass's life. If he had still been in Nikšić with his unit the rest of his war would have been very different. He could have found himself with the partisans. He could have been killed on the hillside with his captain and his sergeant. He could have been deported to Germany and died in a labour camp. Yet, because he was travelling home to Italy on the very day of the Italian surrender, events took an entirely different course.

By the time the train steamed into the little Bosnian town of Višegrad, it was already getting dark. Višegrad was the childhood home of Ivo Andrić, Yugoslavia's only winner of the Nobel Prize for Literature. His best-known novel *Bridge on the Drina* deals with the bitter complexities of life in the Balkans where once Catholics and Orthodox Christians, Jews and Muslims had lived together peacefully, but no longer could. It described Višegrad through the story of the town's bridge, built by the Ottomans in 1566 to connect Bosnia with the world. Later it became a bitterly contested frontier crossing, dynamited by the Austrians who had built the railway that brought Sottsass to the town. Half a century after Andrić finished his book a modern Serb militia lead by a psychopath named Milan Lukic butchered several hundred Bosnian Muslim civilians. His trademark was to drop the bodies of his victims from the bridge into the river.

On 8 September at 18:30, the BBC broadcast General Eisenhower's announcement of Italy's surrender. An hour and a quarter later, the Italian Prime Minister, Pietro Badoglio, confirmed news of the armistice that Italy's King Vittorio Emanuele III had signed secretly five days earlier. Sottsass's message home was stamped at 19:45 by the military telegraph office. He had no means of knowing how Italy's former allies would react to the news of the surrender. However, he had seen the German machine guns at each end of his train as it came to a halt, and it made him think twice about the Leica that he had slung around his neck. When a German soldier boarded the train, and asked him as the only German-speaking Italian officer to follow him to the station master's office, it was not, he thought, the right time to look like a tourist. He paused and handed his camera to the first of his men that he saw, saying 'keep it for me until I get back.'

While the crew on the locomotive footplate went on stoking the fire box with coal to keep up steam, Sottsass climbed down from the little train that was built to such a narrow gauge (in order to thread through impossible mountain terrain) it had the proportions of a toy. He found the station full of Germans with their rifles pointed at him. The colonel in charge told him with brutal simplicity that he was a prisoner. 'From today, Italy is no longer allied with Germany. Italy has sided with our enemies. You are our prisoner, put down your weapon and get back on the train.'

The idea of attempting to escape came and went in an instant. The knowledge that the whole train was in range of the German machine guns was enough to convince Sottsass to do as he was told and to go back and explain to the other Italians that they were now prisoners. From being a few days away from what might have seemed like the relative safety of Turin, he was suddenly in the midst of a level of uncertainty even greater than fighting Tito's partisans in the mountains.

Turin was also in turmoil. The Allies were bombing the city's factories. Strikes against the war had broken out and food was scarce. On the day of Mussolini's arrest six weeks earlier, the Fascist Party's headquarters in the city had been set on fire, and angry crowds stopped the fire brigade from getting close. The German army had already started to appear on the streets, some in helmets marked with the words 'Viva il Duce'. The Wehrmacht was based in the Hotel Astoria and on 8 September the SS commandeered the Hotel Nazionale.

Sottsass's train crawled back to Sarajevo under the guns of the Germans who had boarded it. Everything had changed in an instant. When Sottsass asked for his camera back he was met with the reply: 'You didn't give me anything, you are no longer an officer, you are like the rest of us, you are a prisoner.'

Some hours later, Sottsass and the other Italians were taken off the train in Sarajevo. They were marched through the city's streets to a jail run by the Ustaša. They were spat upon by hostile crowds as they went. To the Germans and their Croat allies, the Italians were cowards and traitors, deserters from the fight who had abandoned their allies.

Sottsass and a dozen other Italians were locked into a single cell. It was a hungry winter for Sarajevo, a city of 350,000, with its supply lines cut by the fighting all around it. The mayor was desperately telegraphing the Croatian capital Zagreb for food and fuel. There was so little to eat that civil servants and factory workers were no longer reporting for work, and the German troops in the city had started a collection for the relief of the starving.

When the jailer came to the Italians' cell, all he brought them to eat was a pail of hot water in which a few vegetables floated. One soldier had been impressed enough by the variety of onion that he found back in Montenegro to take a sackful back for his mother to plant in her garden in Italy. He shared them, cooked in a helmet over a fire made from burning newspapers.

In his pack, Sottsass had a large bottle of cologne and a bagful of the same variety of Macedonian tobacco that three months later was going to buy him a meal at the Hotel Sacher in Vienna. He knew that it would make him friends in Turin where cigarettes had been reduced to factory sweepings and scraps of newspaper. Sottsass rolled a cigarette, lit up and shared some of the rest of his tobacco around the cell.

'When they came that evening they told us we would be shot in the morning, but they didn't do it. Perhaps they only said it to make us feel bad, or perhaps not. Perhaps they really had meant to do it.'

The Germans had had three months to plan for an Italian collapse, as had the partisans. When the end did come there was a rush to seize Italian equipment and Italian-held territory before the other side could take them. The second priority was to recruit, or to disarm the Italian soldiers left stranded by the armistice.

Sottsass remembers that he and his men were ordered into the grey cement courtyard of their cellblock, along with all the other Italian prisoners. 'We were asked if we were ready to work for the Germans, or not. If the answer was no, we would be sent to a concentration camp in Germany.'

It was a scene that was being repeated all across Montenegro, Croatia, Bosnia, Albania and Greece. No divisional commander agreed to join the Germans. Many soldiers from the two Alpini divisions in Montenegro took the decision to join the partisans and styled themselves the Garibaldi Partisan Division.

In the courtyard of the prison in Sarajevo, the Italians debated how to respond to the German ultimatum. 'We talked about it for a while, and then all of us, me included, decided to work for the Germans. In fact not all, one soldier stood up and said, "I am going to the camp".' It was the same soldier, a veteran anarchist, to whom Sottsass had given his camera for safekeeping in Višegrad.

After the Germans accepted their undertakings, Sottsass, a sergeant, and twenty men were moved out of the jail to the barracks that the Austrians had built when they controlled Sarajevo, a sprawling white complex on a hill overlooking the city. Sottsass remembered it as full of marching, drilling Ustaša, boots stamping and rifle butts crashing. The Italians were there as labourers, to work in the stores, carrying, sorting, cleaning and packing. Sottsass's squad was met by a Wehrmacht captain. He wanted to know if any of them spoke German. It turned out that he was an Austrian. When Sottsass told him that though he was an Italian, he had been born in Innsbruck, his conditions improved immediately. Sottsass got a cell of his own, with a basin, a tap and its own lavatory even if it was no more than a hole in the floor. Sottsass had been lucky once again.

The days passed, and the Germans began to treat Sottsass and the other Italians not so much as prisoners, but as if they were civilian workers. He was allowed out of the barracks at night, at first under supervision, then on his own, wearing a German armband over his Italian uniform. This was how he met the third of his wartime lovers. With ecumenical open-mindedness, after Leonora the Serb communist and Geka the Bosnian Muslim he encountered Boba 'Bobitza' Vizdal, the Catholic Croat in Sarajevo. He saw her for the first time sitting alone in a darkened Viennese-style café. It was, Sottsass wrote, 'almost empty, just full of tables and chairs.' She was on her own, 'young and with beautiful lips and dancing eyes'.

Sottsass found in women some protection from the brutality of the conflict. He called them soft and vulnerable. They offered him, even in their vulnerability, a sense of safety in the midst of the constant insecurity of war: 'Bobitza was a soft girl. She had a sad air, a little frightened looking; she protected me in the cloud of her fragrant, moist femininity, she protected me with her unhappiness and with her uncertain future.' He was attracted even though, as he would later say, he knew that she was no saint.

> She cooked for me with so much sugar. She cooked me
> spaghetti with sugar and fried breadcrumbs. She even
> put sugar in the salad [...] She took me some nights to her
> house, not for money, which I didn't have, but perhaps
> because she preferred to make love with a young man,

than with a fat German colonel. That's how it was. Perhaps she took pity on me, on my youth, more or less patriotic, a semi-prisoner of the Germans. Well, I drank a lot, and smoked a lot. I was nervous, I was very thin, I had long hair, and was very pale. I seemed like the perfect romantic figure of the defeated young hero. Everything was temporary. We could expect nothing of the future. Every day was just that day. Every night was just that night. Anything else had to wait. We made love as the only and the last hope, in the kitchen, on a kind of sofa. Bobitza had her own room with a bed, but it seemed too far. We were always in too much of a hurry to take each other in our arms. My curiosity had not yet ventured into the complex quagmire of political thought, in fact I did not understand. Politics for me was, and perhaps still is, a concept too big for my brain. Perhaps it was too risky. It was physically too risky, it did not allow me to experience the world, to smell, to touch, to listen, didn't allow me tears, solitude, didn't allow me the escape of ignorance, or of laziness, not even the sweet escape of idleness.

The politicians told me what to do, how to dress, how I should look, what I should eat, when I should walk slowly, and when I should run, they told me what was good and what was bad, they didn't let me understand, they didn't let me judge, they didn't let me breathe, they didn't let me hope, but they sent me to war.

Five weeks after the armistice, the German army snatched Mussolini from jail, and on 16 October 1943, the Repubblica Sociale Italiana and the Third Reich signed the Rastenburg Protocol. Mussolini was given German consent to raise an army. A network of training camps was established in Germany, and the fascists set about establishing four new Italian divisions. In the first week of 1943, Sottsass volunteered for the Alpini Monterosa Division. Of its 20,000 men, just 4,000 were, like Sottsass, veterans of the old Italian army. 'I didn't say much, it was the way to get back to Italy.'

However, it was clearly not a decision that Sottsass took lightly. Two days before the end of the year in a letter to his parents sent by way of the

German Feldpost, he asked them: 'Write me something about Italy, of the political news — I want to know about the army of the RSI, then if you can, tell me something of the Ministry of War. If you can, please send me a parcel: watercolours and pencils.' If he had already made up his mind what to do, he did not say so in the letter. A week later, in a letter dated 7 January 1944, he enclosed a copy of the declaration that he made in his own handwriting confirming that he had volunteered to serve in the army of the Repubblica Sociale Italiana: 'The undersigned lieutenant of the Alpine Engineers, Ettore Sottsass, volunteer worked for Feldpost 45960. I am answering the call by the government to join the forces of the Italian Fascist Republic.'

Sottsass joined the Monterosa Division because he believed that, if he was to have any chance of getting home to Italy, he had no choice. It was fighting for Mussolini, or being sent to a concentration camp. Only a tiny fraction of Italy's soldiers trapped in German-held territory by the surrender of September 1943 made the same choice. So many more preferred to fight against the Germans. In Cephalonia, the Italian garrison spent two weeks in a doomed struggle with their former allies. More than 10,000 of them were killed in combat, murdered by the Germans, or drowned when the prison ship taking them to captivity hit a mine. In Montenegro, 40,000 soldiers from the Alpini, many among them from Sottsass's own Taurinense Division elected to fight alongside the Yugoslav partisans.

The chaotic Italian surrender exemplified the heartless incompetence of the Italian state under royalist as well as fascist control. The Fascist Grand Council had deposed Mussolini in July. The king arrested him, without having an effective strategy for withdrawing from the war, and took six weeks to announce an armistice that gave Germany time to prepare to turn on Italy. The king fled Rome, and German vengeance, for the safety of Allied-occupied Bari. He and his government abandoned 700,000 Italian soldiers outside Italy's borders to their fate. Except for the capital ships of the Italian fleet and the planes of the air force, there was no preparation of any kind in Rome for the surrender. All Pietro Badoglio said in his broadcast to Italy's soldiers on 8 September was that they should stop fighting. He had given the army no warning. They had no time to organize any defence against the Germans who surrounded them. Who would risk their life for such a regime?

Sottsass refers more than once in his writings to two soldiers he knew well in Montenegro. Both his captain and his quartermaster refused to take the German offer. As a result of that decision, they died on a hillside in Montenegro.

Their names were Eridano Ruga, the company commander, and Arnaldo Trezzi, the quartermaster sergeant. As Sottsass described it, they took the decision to walk home unarmed and were killed, cut full of holes by German machine-gun bullets. Trezzi is one of the people that Sottsass included in his extraordinary tribute, the fifty dead friends, mentors and inspirations that he drew for his 1999 lithograph, their faces recognizable even under Sottsass's black pencil scribble.

The records of the Garibaldi Partisan Division tell a story that does not quite reflect the myth of a heroic resistance. They show that the two men were killed in action against the Germans. Trezzi died on 17 September, Ruga two days later, both of them in Cevo, a hamlet in the hills above Kotor on the road down to the coast and a ship back to Italy. Sottsass doesn't spell out exactly how it was that he survived the war while they did not, but the claim that they were members of the partisan division is not precisely true. It was only some weeks after the deaths of Ruga and Trezzi that the remnants of the Taurinense and Venezia Alpini Divisions reconstituted themselves as partisans, and started to fight alongside Tito's men against the Nazis. It is an event commemorated with a modest memorial, inscribed both in Italian and Serbo-Croatian, in Pljevlja.

It took several weeks before Sottsass was sent to the Monterosa training camp in Germany after his letter to his parents. He had been transferred from Sarajevo to Mostar, and remained there until March 1944. To get to Germany, he had to spend a night in Sarajevo.

Sottsass went back to his Croat lover for the last time. 'I went to see Bobitza. Her widowed mother let us sleep in her double bed, while she was in the kitchen.' The following morning, with Sottsass heading for Germany, Bobitza went with him to the station to say goodbye. The platform was full of Germans looking suspiciously at an unarmed Italian officer with a long black feather in his hat, embracing a tall beautiful woman. It was a moment that Sottsass would remember for the rest of his life.

> At the moment it came for me to leave on the train, she
> looked at me and asked very quietly, 'Will you give me
> your address in Italy?' There was a short silence. 'I don't
> know it, my parents are no longer in the city.' And there
> she stayed on her own, she gave me her love, all that she
> had to give, and I couldn't even give her an address. It
> was like a film, the train started to move, and Bobitza got

smaller and smaller ever more immobile ever further away.
I was also on my own, but at least I had an address.

Half a century later, in *Scritto di Notte*, Sottsass wrote, 'I believed when she disappeared from the window of the train she turned, walked down the station platform, went home, climbed the stairs, sat down in the kitchen and waited.' In fact Sottsass did not forget her. In one of his wartime letters to his parents, he gives them details of her address in Sarajevo, and suggests that they write to her, in German, to thank her for her kindness to him. She had fed him during their time together when there was so little to eat that the interned Italians were on the brink of starvation. She had put sugar in the pasta that she cooked for him that brought back the flavours of his childhood in the mountain of the Tyrol.

Sottsass took the narrow-gauge train to Belgrade, then changed onto the main line for Vienna, where he changed trains again. When he finally got to the Monterosa training camp, he was issued with a new uniform to replace the one that he had worn continuously for the past four months. It involved the same soft felt Capello of the Alpini, with the same raven's feather that he had always worn. But the badge was different: the eagle of the Repubblica Sociale Italiana, and not the insignia of the Royal Army. The insignia on the collar was the Roman sword of Mussolini's republic, not the star that signified the Kingdom of Italy.

Sottsass refused to join the renamed Fascist Party of the Social Republic, rather than the Fascist Party of the Kingdom of Italy. Rodolfo Graziani, Mussolini's army chief, attempted to enshrine the apolitical nature of the military in its doctrine, in an effort to give the new state some kind of claim to legitimacy. Nevertheless all the officers of the old Royal army joining the Monterosa were obliged to put their name to the following declaration:

> The undersigned hereby declares that he is ready to fight
> as an armed volunteer with the Italian forces being
> established against the common enemy of the Italian Social
> Republic, and Greater Germany. I am a supporter of the
> Italian republican fascists, and voluntarily declare that
> I am ready to take arms to fight for the Duce and the new
> Italian army, without reservations under the German
> high command against the common enemies of the Duce's
> RSI and the Greater German Reich.

Sottsass and the other veterans repatriated from the Balkans were there to stiffen the nineteen-year-olds called up from those areas of Italy still controlled by Mussolini. Despite the propaganda claiming that the Monterosa would restore Italy's honour, and despite the promise of modern equipment, food rations in the training camps were minimal. Contemporary diaries record recruits scavenging for scraps of potato peelings and rotten cabbage. Discipline was brutal. On one occasion five Monterosa soldiers were caught trying to desert from the camp. They were brought back to face a court martial, lined up in front of the division, forced to dig their own graves, and then shot.

Germany spent a year training its élite troops. The Italians were rushed through in five months, or in some cases far less time. They were trained in house-to-house fighting, in field craft, in assault on fortified positions, and in German tactics and communications.

For Mussolini to be seen to have any kind of credibility, he had to put a visibly Italian army into the field against the advancing British and Americans as soon as could be managed. On 16 July 1944 he reviewed a march past of the 19,000 soldiers of the Monterosa Division at Munzingen.

Sottsass, as a veteran of the war in the Balkans, was back in Italy after a few weeks in Germany in his new uniform and once again equipped with his personal weapons, while the rest of the division completed their basic training. On the last day of March 1944, Sottsass wrote to reassure his parents that he had reported to his new base, and had joined the Alpini of the Republican army. 'Guess who's our commander — it's Colonel Rella. The old Italy is dead, and there is a new one which will endure and live.' Sottsass's role in the Monterosa was as a logistics officer. His job was to distribute supplies to the front line: chocolate, soap, tins of food, razor blades, matches and ammunition.

After the Monterosa left Germany, on their return to Italy they were greeted not as the rescuers of Italian pride but in many places with silence or contempt. In Peschiera del Garda, an eighteen-year-old was killed by the Alpini for insulting them. The Germans remained deeply suspicious and insisted on careful monitoring of the RSI's soldiers. Despite the efforts of the SS and the military police, more than 1,000 Monterosa troops had deserted within two months of their return to Italy. Up to twenty-five percent of its men had laid down their weapons and fled before the end of the year. On 15 December 1944 the Monterosa divisional HQ issued a caution to all its men, warning them all against joining other units 'such as the Blackshirts etc., an act that will be treated as desertion'. It was not an option that Sottsass considered at the time.

Sottsass was based initially at Chiavari on the relatively quiet Ligurian coast, in the Gulf of Genoa between Nervi and Levanto. The Germans could not be sure where the expected Anglo-American landings would come and needed to guard their flank as they fought off the Allied troops moving up the Italian peninsula at the Gothic line, the defensive line drawn from Pisa to Pesaro. Monterosa manpower allowed the Germans to move their own troops up to the Gothic line.

Sottsass wrote to his parents of his pride in his comrades in the Monterosa, repeating the Republic of Salò's slogan in one letter: '*La Divisione Monterosa é, e rimanerà una divisione di ferro*' ('The division is, and will remain, a division of iron'). The Monterosa was, Sottsass told his parents, the best that the new army had. He was perhaps trying to maintain his own spirits as well as theirs.

When the Allied invasion came, it was actually on the Côte d'Azur on 15 August. With no imminent threat to Liguria, the Monterosa Division was moved away from the coast, and sent to support the Germans on the Gothic line, confronting the Allies as they drove up the centre of Italy. Sottsass was posted to a supply depot in the Garfagnana area of the Tuscan mountains.

Sottsass and his men were charged with supplying the Alpini front line dug in near the summit of a hill from where they could see almost all the way to the sea. Sottsass found a group of abandoned huts half sunk into the ground and established a supply dump. The snow and wind had scoured the huts clean. Sottsass slept more or less on the ground in the stable. His men were in the adjacent hut. According to Sottsass, 'the light was great. I felt good, I felt really good, I was on my own.' The calm was broken one morning when he was woken by the sound of gunfire. He put on his trousers: 'I hurriedly grabbed my braces, I could see a British Spitfire, and the face of the young pilot who was shooting at me.' Sottsass took shelter behind a huge rock, and survived.

The supply dump was replenished once a week. When stores arrived, Sottsass would take them up to the men in the trenches on the mountain top. During this period, the American artillery kept up a continual barrage, but the shells usually burst far below the trenches or passed over the summit into the other side of the valley. 'We climbed up with the van, accompanied by the whistle of shells that went over our heads and exploded in the distance. But we were better off than the Alpini in the trenches. They were mountain kids, or country kids, or suburban kids, who didn't understand what was happening.'

Just before Christmas, a mixed force of Monterosa Italians and Germans counter-attacked against the advancing Americans. They achieved an initial success, pushing back the Allies several kilometres, taking prisoners and capturing supplies. The response was ferocious. On the ground, Indian troops pushed back the advance. The American air force launched wave after wave of attacks to crush the Germans and Italians. It was this counter-attack that brought Sottsass the closest to death that he had yet come.

Sottsass's supply dump was next to a strategic bridge. He heard the sound of American bombers in the air and took shelter under the truck. The rest of his men hid in a clump of trees next to the bridge. Sottsass emerged after the bombs had fallen to find that although the Americans had missed the bridge, his men had been wiped out. Sottsass was taken to a field hospital and had trouble breathing. All they could give him was a flask of grappa. What Sottsass remembered most vividly was the strange white cloud that hung over the bombed site and the curious stench of burnt flesh.

The Americans came back again and again with bombs and machine-gun fire. Finally Sottsass and his men buried the dead, and he took the decision to find somewhere less exposed. One of his men had recently become en-gaged to a local girl. She had told him about a railway tunnel to the north of Garfagnana, on the line south to Lucca that ran 100 metres into the hillside. With the front line cutting across the tracks just a kilometre away there were no trains running. It seemed like a refuge in which to hide. Just before Christmas 1944, he moved his men into the tunnel and built two barricades in the exact centre. The troops spent the winter of 1944–45 there. 'All those months, we didn't change our clothes, day or night.' That is how it was for the whole winter, the Alpini in the cold, in the trenches, looking at the enemy and at the sea in the distance. And Sottsass, with the rest of the survivors, almost always in the dark in the railway tunnel, until as he put it, 'slowly the tunnel mouth became a clear blue sky with clouds flying north and the woods became green'.

In his letters home, Sottsass describes losing all sense of time and place living in that dark tunnel, with only the radio to connect them to the outside world with its random snatches of voices from near and far. It was an experi-ence of claustrophobic isolation that Sottsass later compared to the time he spent desperately ill in a Californian hospital in 1962, unable to move or to go out, reliant on scraps of information from his bedside radio to keep track of the world. In a letter dated 6 January 1945, Sottsass wrote:

This is the after Christmas letter. Its OK now, this is written
by the light of my candle inside my wooden barricade,

inside my railway tunnel, my very long railway tunnel.
We have our stove, our bunks, we even have armchairs.
Slowly, slowly, we will make it more comfortable.

We worked two days and two nights to build it,
and it was finished yesterday after a week in which
we slept in the open, or almost. It was the first night that
we slept inside, and in the warm. We spent Christmas
in a ruined house, amid the stench and the fire of war.
Our hair was full of dust, our eyes were sad because
we had just buried our fallen comrades.

We had said goodbye to those who had been killed.
It was only after nightfall that we could say goodbye to
the dead and the dying. The dead had sung with us, they
had drunk wine with us.

We were machine-gunned from the air in the
morning, and bombed and machine-gunned again, twice.
We resisted. On Christmas Eve, there was the thunder of
artillery from nearby mountains.

Two weeks later, Sottsass wrote again:

I am losing track of time. Your letters are getting scarce;
not more than every ten days, perhaps it's fifteen since
I have had any news from you. I and my comrades have
not had news for some time. Like me, they are alone
and far from home. In this sort of prison which is our little
barricade, in the dark air of the tunnel. We rarely go
outside, only at night, and not often then. We are slowly
losing the sense of time.

Of things, of happenings that only reach us by the
radio, tuning the radio, we hear music from a long way
off. Strange noises, other voices, close and from a very long
way away, of languages unknown and known. The world
is big and strange.

As the snow melted in the spring of 1945, it was clear that the British,
the Americans and their allies were going to be able to move north and take

the war into Germany. Sottsass didn't yet know that the Russians were closing in on Berlin, or that the war was coming to an end. The Italians and the Germans began pulling back from their defensive positions towards the rapidly shrinking heartland of Mussolini's Italy.

> There was talk that the Germans had a new weapon,
> the V2, that was their last hope, but at the same
> time, there was also talk that the English had a new
> engine that would make their aircraft much faster.
> Neither affected us much, but I was happy when we
> were ordered to retreat to Piedmont.

Sottsass and his men pulled back from the mountains down to the plains in a mixed Italian and German convoy, his unit riding in a lorry on the road between Genoa and Turin behind a German motorcycle escort with a young lieutenant driving and an Austrian officer in the sidecar. The convoy was caught at Villanova d'Asti in a partisan ambush, coming under fire from a group of insurgents hidden on top of an embankment on the right-hand side of the road. The truck slammed into the side of the road, and came to a stop; the driver and the Germans in the motorcycle were dead. Sottsass was hit, but not seriously. There was some blood, but the bullet had ricocheted off the truck's engine before passing through his boot. Sottsass crawled out of the wreck of the truck as the partisans kept shooting and the shell-shocked Alpini fired back with their rifles. Sottsass saw a culvert on the other side of the road hidden from the partisans by the crashed truck. He was able to crawl through it to escape. Others in the convoy were not so fortunate.

There were still plenty of fascist sympathizers in the area. They found Sottsass and took him to a hospital where the wound was cleaned and bandaged, and he was given an anti-tetanus injection. Later he found himself riding in the sidecar of another German motorcycle that took him to Turin.

The last winter of the war was particularly harsh in Turin. Temperatures reached eleven degrees below freezing, heating fuel was running out and there was no glass to fix windows blown out by bombing. Germans were trying to seize the production lines in the factories, there was mass unemployment and the constant fear of deportation to forced labour in Germany.

In the absence of his parents, Sottsass went to Fernanda Pivano's home on the Corso Vinzaglio and rang the bell. War had already come to Turin's city centre, the nearby barracks had been bombed, its basements used as shelters. The previous summer, when Sottsass was in Liguria, four hostages had been executed on the corner of the Corso Vinzaglio and the via Cernaia in retaliation for the killing of a non-commissioned officer from the RSI armoured division. The hostages were driven to the site on the back of a truck and hanged in front of a small crowd. The bodies remained dangling from a makeshift gallows next to a tram stop overnight, while two more partisans were executed on a nearby bridge.

'Fernanda came to the door and I opened my eyes and opened my mouth.' Sottsass remembered. 'Nothing came out, I could think of nothing to say. "You smell like a goat," Fernanda told me. She opened the door, made me take a bath and made me put on her brother's pyjamas.'

Sottsass left the apartment some days later, with his uniform freshly laundered and ironed, and presented himself at Turin's military headquarters. He was interviewed by a colonel. Even at this very late stage when Hitler and Mussolini were obviously about to be defeated Sottsass was still not ready to desert. He was given the name of a military post near Ivrea and told to report there. He saluted and turned to go, when the colonel called him back with a question: 'You have long hair Sottsass, when are you going get it cut?'

Graziani, commander of the Salò army, ordered what was meant to be fascism's last stand. The remains of the army were to fall back to the left bank of the River Po and then to take up a new defensive line along the Alps. The Monterosa Division, now down to less than half its original strength, was to concentrate on one of four bases, including the arms dump near Ivrea.

On the way there Sottsass knew that he would pass through Rivarolo Canavese, where there was a vermouth distillery that belonged to a family called Grassotti. Sottsass had met them in 1938 before the war. They had a son called Aldo and a daughter Josephine, whose architect fiancé had been killed in the Spanish Civil War. Pivano had told Sottsass that Aldo Grassotti was a partisan, sometimes hiding in the mountains with other fighters, sometimes back at home to collect intelligence. Sottsass stopped at the house and was asked in for lunch. During the course of the meal, Grassotti suggested Sottsass come with him to the mountains. It was the beginning of what would be an important relationship for Sottsass after the war. He would later design posters and exhibition stands for the family product and furniture for their son.

Sottsass replied that he would need to think about it, but he had already stopped seeing himself as an officer of the Monterosa. He and the few men that he felt responsible for had already lost contact with the divisional command. They knew nothing about why they were being sent to the post near Ivrea or what they were meant to be doing there.

Sottsass went back to the Grassotti house. Two nights later, Aldo came back for him in an old convertible car and they set off for the mountains. Some kilometres into the dark, they drove into an ambush and found themselves being shot at with tracer bullets 'They were beautiful to look at,' Sottsass remembered. 'We could not tell if they were fascist, partisan or German bullets.'

The car ended up in the ditch. In the darkness Sottsass lost his guide and set off to walk in the opposite direction from which the shots had come. Still in his Monterosa uniform, and in fear that if he met the partisans they would kill him as a fascist or that if he met the fascists they would kill him as a deserter, Sottsass walked through the dark landscape. Eventually he found himself in a village piazza. In the blackout, he could make out the dark figures of five men, all in black, sitting outside a bar that was shuttered and closed. To judge by their uniforms they were fascists. They asked Sottsass no questions about what he was doing (perhaps out of respect for the Alpini uniform that had meant so much to Italy in World War I) and showed him the way to get back to Rivarolo Canavese and the Grassotti house. When Sottsass arrived, he found Aldo there already. The family called Pivano who found Sottsass a doctor.

Sottsass's war was coming to an end, but not before Turin went through a final bloody spasm. When the German army withdrew, diehard fascist snipers stayed and from behind shuttered upper windows in the attics, they shot at partisans and civilians in the streets below. There were hundreds of deaths. Then on 28 April 1945, Giuseppe Solaro, the last fascist commissioner for Turin, was caught, and on the following day, tried and hanged on the same street on which the four partisans had been executed the previous year. It was the Corso Vinzaglio, the street on which Pivano's family lived, where six years earlier, she had her first awkward encounter with Sottsass. Shots were fired into Solaro's lifeless body, then his corpse was loaded onto a truck and driven to the banks of the River Po where it was disposed of. It took another week for the killing finally to come to an end in the city.

Post-War to America

101

Before there was a new constitution, before there was an elected government, even before Italy was fully at peace, its architects had already plunged into an attempt to define how best to rebuild their country. Turin's streets had not yet been cleared of rubble and unexploded ordnance when an influential group of architects declared that to be truly modern, design had to be not only functional, but explicitly anti-fascist too. Sottsass, his father and twenty-two other architects in Turin joined this national initiative. They signed the manifesto of the Associazione per l'Architettura Organica (the APAO, or Association for Organic Architecture) on 22 October 1945. The manifesto was inspired by Bruno Zevi (the architect from Rome whom Ettore Sottsass had first encountered seven years earlier on their officer-training course in the mountains), but tailored to the particular sensibilities of Turin.

None of them — not Sottsass, not his father, nor their colleagues — had work. And, in the chaos at the end of the war, there was no immediate possibility of any. However this did not stop them from signing the manifesto, or from talking about how they would build if they got the chance, even as they struggled to feed themselves and to keep warm in a freezing winter. They named the Turin section of the association in memory of Giuseppe Pagano, their martyred colleague, murdered just six months earlier in a death camp across the border in Austria. The tribute was a political gesture, but it also reflected sympathy for Pagano's particular approach to architecture.

When Pagano died on 22 April 1945 in Mauthausen-Gusen, the extermination camp built with the slave labour of political prisoners from massive blocks of stone and deliberately designed to intimidate, Sottsass had finally abandoned the disintegrating remnants of the Monterosa Division. Pagano was a complex figure who, during his days as an ardent fascist, had worked in the prevailing Rationalist idiom. However in 1936, he had also organized an exhibition of vernacular Italian architecture at the Milan Triennale with Guarniero Daniel, which would eventually set the course for a post-war reaction against the ruthless symmetry of Rationalism, understood by then as undesirably anti-democratic.

The APAO manifesto said a lot about the state of Italy, and the contortions that it required of its intellectuals if they were to adapt to its rapidly changing ideological landscape. Sottsass's father — so recently congratulated by the Partito Nazionale Fascista's Federazione dei Fasci di Combattimento of Turin for his 'fervour and nobility' and his faithfulness 'to the fascist spirit' — and his son were ready to sign the APAO manifesto. It is a statement that begins as follows:

> The origins of Modern architecture, in which I believe, are to be found essentially in functionalism, even as it has evolved into an organic architecture. I remain convinced that functionalism is the true path of Modern architecture, and not the styling of Neoclassicism, nor petty provincialism.
>
> Organic architecture is simultaneously a social, technical and artistic activity. It is directed towards creating the context for a new, democratic civilization.
>
> Organic architecture means an architecture based on human scale, on the spiritual, psychological and material needs of man. It is therefore, the antithesis of the monumentalism that serves the creation of state myths.
>
> Inseparable from this architectural principle is a belief in the general principles of political and social justice. Political liberty and social justice are indispensible elements in building a democratic society, a constitution that guarantees its citizens freedom of speech, of the press, of association, and of religion, and universal suffrage. I believe in the international cooperation of peoples.

At the time that Sottsass senior and junior signed these words, Italy was physically devastated and psychologically traumatized by the fall of fascism, by a civil war, by the violent passage of an invading Allied army, and the protracted and painful expulsion of the Nazis. Once the killing had stopped, it took more than a year for the king to abdicate, and for his son to be deposed in a deeply divisive national referendum that adopted a post-fascist republican constitution in May 1946.

On Italy's eastern border, the advance of Tito's partisans into the suburbs of Trieste had turned the city into an international zone, partitioned between the British and the Americans on one side, and the Yugoslavs on the other, in much same way as Berlin and Vienna were divided at the same time.

General de Gaulle only withdrew his forces from val d'Aosta when the Americans threatened to cut off his supplies. The Americans and the Vatican worried that Italy would elect a communist government. The country was still overshadowed by extra-judicial killings and the violent settling of old scores that continued for many months after the war ended. Even Gio Ponti was spoken of as a target for assassination because of his ties with fascism. However, bleak though the situation seemed, Italy was on the starting line of the most sustained burst of economic development in its modern history. The backward economy that Mussolini failed to modernize was, at last, about to embark on two decades of continuous growth that would propel the country into the modern world.

Italy's GDP doubled between 1950 and 1962. In the same period, as many as seven million people moved from its poverty stricken rural south into the industrial triangle in the north defined by the cities of Turin, Genoa and Milan. It was this remarkable transition (the closest comparison that Europe has seen to the wave of development in China at the end of the twentieth century) that fuelled the start of Sottsass's independent career.

During *il miracolo economico*, Italy went from being a low-cost manufacturer to an economy that used design to create premium products it could sell around the world. Fiat would stop building the faintly comic 'Topolino' in 1947, and move towards the formal brilliance and technical innovation of the Cinquecento in 1959. Italy began to make the Lamborghinis and Ferraris that became international bywords for glamour. Pietro Cardin had to leave Italy to become Pierre Cardin in Paris. Valentino also started his career in France, but went home in 1959 to lay the foundations for a global Italian fashion brand. Sottsass went from building workers' housing and designing fruit bowls made from knitted wire, to being called in by Olivetti to design a computer in the space of twelve years.

But this transformation did not come all at once. In the hunger of the immediate aftermath of the war, Sottsass was ready to try just about anything. He had a press card, naming him as a photo-reporter for the weekly magazine *Epoca*. He went back to Luigi Spazzapan's regular table in the Bar Patria in Turin, and took part in a number of group shows. Sottsass was one of the artists who exhibited in *'Arte Astratta e Concreta'* ('Abstract and Concrete Art'), the exhibition that opened in Milan's Palazzo Reale in January 1947, at which the Movimento Arte Concreta was launched. It was inaugurated by Max Bill (a direct link to the Bauhaus and Wassily Kandinsky who had taught him there) and featured work by Max Huber and Bruno Munari, figures who, like Sottsass, were able to span the gap between art and design. For Italy the exhibition was a departure. Mussolini's attitudes to the visual arts had been ambiguous. There were thugs and philistines in the party who demanded simple-minded propaganda, but there had also been real artists and architects who were able to operate undisturbed under fascism. Gio Ponti had been encouraged by the fascist regime and even awarded the 50,000 lire Mussolini Prize in 1935. Mario Radice (the father of Barbara, who would later marry Sottsass) worked on a remarkable series of murals for the Casa del Fascio in Como designed by Giuseppe Terragni. He was traumatized by seeing them destroyed after the war because he had been obliged to include an image of il Duce. His daughter remembers him drawing and re-drawing versions of it to show how it would have been without the image of the dictator. Giorgio Morandi was both a member of the party, and a painter on the edge of elegant and refined abstraction.

But the Concrete Art exhibition was different from previous exercises in avant-garde art in Italy. For the first time a substantial collection of non-figurative art was on public display in support of a new ideological position. Sottsass had a solo exhibition the following year in Lugano. He produced a sculptural assemblage of metal rods and wire with a vigour that seemed far removed from the vernacular inspiration behind the architecture he was designing at the same time. He was also working as a designer, and it was in this role that he was invited to submit work for the Milan Triennale, alongside Anna Castelli Ferrieri, Achille Castiglioni and many others. It was work that reflected the rhythms that he was exploring in his art.

Ernesto Nathan Rogers and then Gio Ponti gave Sottsass the chance to write for *Domus*. The fees were not going to keep him in comfort, but the bylines made him immediately visible and apparently important. Sottsass's relationship with Rogers was difficult. Rogers saw himself as an intellectual, and had a way of condescending to Sottsass, as well as to Gio Ponti, his professional rival as an editor and an architect. He tended to characterize their work as no more than decorative. Ponti had established *Domus* in 1928, but lost control to the printer-turned-publisher Gianni Mazzocchi in 1941. After the war, Mazzocchi briefly appointed Rogers editor from 1946–7. Under his command *Domus* became a more narrowly architectural magazine, a shift that was not a commercial success and Ponti returned as editor in 1948.

Sottsass's relationship with Ponti was much warmer; the two men clearly liked each other. Ponti gave Sottsass a platform in *Domus*, and helped him with introductions to potential clients. During those early post-war years, Sottsass designed exhibitions for trade fairs, the conventional standby of Italian architects in need of work. Aldo Grassotti, the friend who had offered Sottsass safe passage to the partisans in the last month of the war, commissioned him for projects for the family vermouth business, a stand at a trade fair, posters, even a book of cocktail recipes, as well as to design furniture for his Turin home.

Sottsass initially worked from the studio in the apartment on the Piazza Vittorio Veneto that he shared with his father, but he then began to divide his time between Turin and Milan. He received a commission to organize a section about craft at the Milan Triennale. Not a great enthusiast for folk art or craft of the kind that Italy was making at the time, he held his nose all the same, and took the job.

He found what he described as a cold, damp and unheated room near the central station in Milan in which to stay when he was not in Turin. The Pirovini sisters ran a trattoria in Milan and were ready to feed the hungry artists who frequented it in exchange for a drawing for the walls, Sottsass among them. Despite his doubts and uncertainty about how to make a living, Sottsass began to make plans. After a meeting with one of Carlo Mollino's clients who suggested that he start an art magazine, he began work on dummies for a current affairs magazine that was modelled on *Life* and would have been called *Il Mezzo Secolo*. It was the first of Sottsass's frequent attempts to make magazines that continued into the 1980s when he produced *Terrazzo*. He was working with Brassaï prints and on ideas for features on Max Bill. Sottsass made dummies that mixed advertising spreads from *Life* featuring lotions that would 'keep hair summer-proofed and handsome' with pictures of Oscar Niemeyer in Brazil. He was interested in the style of contemporary glossy American magazines — from the vantage point of an Italy wrecked by war, they seemed to provide a keyhole view into an affluent and sophisticated other world.

Massive wartime destruction made the rebuilding of Italy a matter of urgency. In Milan this materialized in part through the construction of a new neighbourhood, masterplanned by Piero Bottoni (a former associate of Pagano) that would be known as Quartiere Triennale 8. This was a demonstration green suburb conceived as the subject of the 1947 Triennale exhibition. The landscaping included a number of mounds carved out of rubble moved from wartime bombsites. Sottsass submitted an unsuccessful design for a competition to build a church for the project. It is a carefully composed rectilinear structure, distinguished by its use of strong colour, and an open-grid tower.

A year later, Sottsass father and son won a 90,000 lire prize for the design of an emergency housing project to be built by the Ministero dell'Assistenza Postbellica Ufficio Provinciale di Milano as part of the INA-Casa project, a nationwide housing plan developed by the Istituto Nazionale delle Assicurazioni (INA), Italy's National Insurance institute. It was an important step forward for Sottsass, and on the strength of it, he opened a studio in Milan at via Giotto 26.

Sottsass had read the book that Pagano wrote to accompany his exhibition on vernacular building, and it was clearly an influence on his first postwar architectural designs. His ideas about what architecture might be in the 1940s reflected those of others of his generation. Lina Bo Bardi, as an editor of *Domus* magazine during the war, wrote about the Mediterranean and the relevance of its vernacular tradition to the present day, in a way that seems closely to reflect Sottsass's own early building projects. His time as a critic at *Domus* in the post-war years gave him the opportunity to examine the work of one of the most distinctive architects of the period, Richard Neutra, albeit only seeing his work in photographs. In his synthesis of modernity, with humble materials, Neutra seemed to be offering a pointer for post-war Italy. Sottsass also went to see the Unité d'habitation, and Le Corbusier's 'Mediterranean' approach resonated with him.

As the Italian economy restarted, Sottsass and his father began working together, and those projects show a decisive shift from the pre-war work of the older man. The formal compositions, marble and the scale dissolve into intimate spaces and humble materials. The shift was not driven only by scarcity, but also had an ideological meaning. And for the elder Sottsass it must have seemed like a return to his work on the reconstruction of the Trentino after World War I.

On a national scale, more than one-third of Italy's architects took part in the INA-Casa project — an initiative intended both to create jobs and to build homes, and also to signal a new approach to creating communities in Italy. Established in 1949 by Amintore Fanfani, the Minister for Labour and Social Security, who had himself once been a member of the Scuola Mistica Fascista alongside Giuseppe Pagano, the scheme depended on the use of Marshall Aid funds and a levy on salaries in order to pay for the building of more than 350,000 working-class homes. INA set up an office in Rome to oversee the project, and drew on the advice of Adriano Olivetti and Adalberto

Libera among others to prepare a design guide for the new homes. It addressed both internal planning principles and contextual issues. The maximum density for INA projects was specified as no more than 500 people to the hectare, and the average height of new homes was specified as three storeys.

To secure commissions under the terms of the programme, architects had to take part in a specimen competition in order to demonstrate their abilities. Those who were successful won a place on the register of officially approved professionals, from which communities undertaking local building projects could select their chosen architects.

Sottsass father and son worked on a number of different projects under the scheme. They designed several buildings in a mining area of Sardinia, and more in Trento, Lombardy and Piedmont. Sottsass's first projects with his father, for low-budget social housing in Sardinia and Lombardy, and his more speculative individual projects all demonstrate promising attempts at finding what he might have defined as a kind of specifically Mediterranean Modernism — that is to say an architecture that owed something to Le Corbusier in his more emotional moods rather than to Walter Gropius. It is work that occupied a well-understood part of the contemporary architectural landscape. Sottsass avoided overarching formal solutions and single monolithic volumes. He attempted to transform simple briefs with sculptural but economical oversailing roofs. He broke up plans into distinct, often discontinuous elements, and used applied screens and exposed rubble to give texture and relief to his facades.

Fernanda Pivano proposed to Sottsass one day in 1948, when he finally told her that he had the chance of a home and setting up a practice in Milan. She was approaching thirty, and her parents were becoming increasingly concerned about her failure to settle down to the conventions of upper middle-class Italian domestic life at what seemed an advanced age. Sottsass did not have the answer she wanted to hear. Instead he asked 'Why get married?' It provoked an immediate rupture and Pivano left him. She took the train to Rome to marry an American officer she had recently met at the military radio station there.

However, the following year Pivano invited Sottsass to come and visit her in Rome. The failure of her first marriage (if indeed it was such) was not an episode that Pivano discusses in her own diaries (divorce was illegal in Italy until 1970), although she does hint at it in the *roman à clef* that she wrote after her divorce from Sottsass.

Sottsass and Pivano were finally married in a civil ceremony in Turin in October 1949, eleven years after they had first met in her parents' overpoweringly bourgeois home on the corso Vinzaglio. In the photographs taken at the time (so poignantly different from the official record of the wartime wedding of Sottsass's parents in the still Austrian mountains) Pivano looked like a glamorous Latin Ingrid Bergman dressed in a fur coat. Sottsass had a slender moustache and an elegant suit and could have passed for Maurice Chevalier. In fact, Sottsass was always thinking about cinematic precedents for the major events that marked his life, from the Chetniks in Montenegro that reminded him of Pancho Villa's bandits onwards. And he owned at least one straw boater.

Pivano was one of Italy's leading literary intellectuals, a translator, an editor and a journalist. Sottsass was still struggling to work out exactly what and who he was. Since the end of the war, he had explored some radically different directions. The connections with Max Bill and his meetings with Brancusi and Picasso in Paris could have propelled him into defining himself as an artist. As he and his father were beginning to make a name for themselves as the architects who were leading the post-war reconstruction of Italy, he was also designing furniture and shops and posters. He wasn't entirely convinced about the long-term significance of any of these roles.

Sottsass and Pivano took their parents and friends for cakes and prosecco in a *pasticceria* after the wedding and then caught the train from the Porta Nuova station back to Milan two hours away. They were by now living together in a flat (for which, Sottsass complained, he had to spend 8,000 lire on a wood-burning stove to keep them warm). So far, theirs had been a complicated, passionate and often difficult relationship and it would be no different after their marriage had been formalized.

Pivano and Sottsass struggled to find a way to live together. Pivano was an accomplished and creative woman, determined to make her own way, but she was also impulsive and melodramatic. She was anxious to leave Turin, which, as she saw it, was a city stuck in its own past as an eighteenth-century provincial court that had never found a new role. Sottsass was ready to go too. For his father, Turin had been a disappointment; he had never achieved all that he had hoped for and had lost the house he had built for himself before the war. For his son, Turin was not a city in which he felt comfortable. However, in the Italy of the 1940s, it was not easy for Sottsass to accept a situation in which Pivano — with her bourgeois family and her doctorate — was better connected and better educated than he was. Her friends were more famous than his. His friends were more interested in her than her friends were interested in talking to him. And he only had the words to communicate at any profound level with the Italian speakers among her circle.

Pivano was about to introduce him to Ernest Hemingway. Sottsass had introduced her to the charismatic, but relatively obscure, Luigi Spazzapan. She would take him to Paris to meet Alice B. Toklas, and through her to secure introductions for Sottsass to Picasso and Brancusi. Sottsass documents all these encounters in photographs. He spent a day in Picasso's company and captured the artist's distant gaze, eyes shaded by a beret. He photographed a young boy with an ink drawing made by Picasso on his bare chest. He photographed Toklas in the apartment in Paris she once shared with Gertrude Stein, smoking and in distracted conversation with Pivano. Both women wore their coats indoors, a reflection of post-war fuel shortages. Toklas's is wool, Pivano has a mink. Sottsass's camera did not fail to take in the walls, thick with Picasso's canvases. Sottsass was having financial difficulties, to the extent that a bailiff arrived one morning to take his furniture in settlement of an unpaid bill. Pivano paid him off.

Pivano also had the connections to introduce him to Arnoldo Mondadori, the publisher for whom she worked, and through him to the most famous man in Italy, Fiat heir Giovanni Agnelli, as well as his brother Giorgio, both of whom commissioned Sottsass to work on interiors for them. Sottsass designed a small apartment for Giovanni Agnelli in Milan, but was on closer terms with his Harvard-educated brother Giorgio, who took little part in the family business and died in a Swiss clinic aged just thirty-five. Giorgio was interested in Sottsass. He liked to question him about the direction that design might take in the future. Could there, for example, ever be a Perspex telephone? And when Sottsass's father was close to death, he introduced him to his own doctor in an effort to help.

Pivano took Sottsass to meet Ernest Hemingway in the mountains in Cortina and then in Venice, and then later to holiday with him in Cuba. She suggests Spencer Tracy and Katharine Hepburn, who were filming *The Old Man and the Sea* at the time, also visited Hemingway while they were there. Pivano would later introduce Sottsass to Allen Ginsberg and the beat poets, who would make Hemingway seem as dated in the world of letters as Frank Lloyd Wright would soon be in the world of architecture.

Sottsass confessed that he could barely understand a word of English when he first met Hemingway. 'I had learned English from reading American comics. The rest that I learned of English and French, I learned from sitting in silence, hour after hour, listening to Fernanda chatting to her English and French friends.' It is not hard to appreciate how this would have made Sottsass feel.

'I tried to start [a] magazine and got close to making it happen, but it was one of the many fuck-ups of my life.' Sottsass recalled in *Scritto di Notte*. Mondadori was interested in publishing it and Agnelli was considering providing the financial backing, but the project came to nothing. 'I said to somebody that the trouble with Italian intellectuals was that they knew nothing about the real world and of course it got back to Mondadori. That was that the end of my dream of the magazine.' There was also Sottsass's relationship with his father to deal with. Sottsass was gradually making the transition from junior partner in the practice to its figurehead. He needed to prove himself, but he wanted to maintain the closeness with his father that he valued so much.

Pivano and Sottsass met Hemingway for the first time in Cortina d'Ampezzo, the ski resort in the mountains above Venice, when Hemingway made his first pilgrimage back to Italy — the scene of his adventures as an ambulance driver in World War I. Hemingway, then aged fifty, and Mary Welsh, a decade younger, who had recently become his fourth wife, arrived in Genoa in October 1948 on a Polish liner. They had brought their Buick convertible with them from America and hired a local driver to chauffeur them to Cortina.

Pivano was working on the first official Italian translation of *A Farewell to Arms*, a book that Mussolini had suppressed because of its less than flattering portrayal of Italy's retreat from the Austrians in World War I. Hemingway invited her to come up to the mountains to see him. Years later, she suggested that Hemingway wrote to her because he heard that she had been jailed by the Nazis for translating his book. Whilst it is true that to be found in possession of a contract to translate a banned book during World War II was dangerous, Pivano herself seems to have suffered only an afternoon's interrogation. However, her brother was beaten severely by Germans under the impression that he was the 'Fernando Pivano' named in a contract to translate the book that had been found in a search of the Rome offices belonging to the publisher Giulio Einaudi.

Meeting Hemingway was, she wrote much later, 'the greatest thrill of my life'. Pivano was thirty-two at the time and no doubt overwhelmed by working with one of the major literary figures of the century. In a letter dated 27 October 1948, Hemingway wrote to Pivano inviting her to come and see him, and telling her that he was feeling at home at the Gritti Palace Hotel, where

'Mr Byron, Mr Browning (the poet, not the gun manufacturer) and Mr D'Annunzio (Gabriele) the poet, playwright, novelist and shit, here all wrote. This makes Mr Papa feel as if he has finally arrived at his proper estate.'

Hemingway had a tendency to call the women who caught his attention 'daughter' and Pivano was no exception. However, it seems the writer's focus during his return to Italy was not Pivano, but the Venetian aristocrat Adriana Ivancich, who was to be the inspiration for Renata in *Across the River and into the Trees*. Jay McInerney, writing in the *New Yorker* in 1995, noted that Pivano was famous as the woman who did not sleep with Hemingway. Nevertheless, Pivano clearly wanted as much of Hemingway's attention as she could get. Her judgement of Ivancich as a knowing and flirtatious young woman who distracted and damaged Hemingway may be correct, even if it is not entirely objective.

Sottsass meanwhile, with his limited command of English, could only sit impotently on the edge of the conversation, nodding and smiling while he took photographs of Hemingway. He might be at the beginning of a successful career as an architect and designer, but there was no way to turn heads on the terrace of the Gritti Palace when Hemingway was holding court, and Sottsass's soon-to-be wife was doing her best to compete with her younger rival for the great writer's attention.

Two years after their first meeting, in January 1950, Hemingway was back in Italy and staying with Mary in Venice at his suite at the Gritti Palace. Hemingway was still working on *Across the River and into the Trees*; the book was not published until September of the same year.

According to Pivano's account, Hemingway called her in the middle of the night, and asked her to come over to read the manuscript. She did so while he consumed several bottles of champagne. 'I finished at dawn,' she wrote later. 'The bottles of champagne were all empty, and in the ice buckets the water had become grey like that in the canals. We spoke a little of the book, then Hemingway threw himself on his bed and I left the room on tiptoe. Of the book we never spoke again.'

Hemingway was remarkably charismatic; he was also a troubling, and even, according to his previous wife Martha Gellhorn, a deranged host, given to breakfasts of gin, champagne and absinthe. An infection from a dust particle caught in his left eye when he was in Cortina d'Ampezzo had horrific results. It spread across his whole face, which swelled into a hideous crust even covering his eyelids. It became so serious that the doctors were worried it might get to his brain. It had to be treated with massive doses of penicillin in the hospital in Padua.

Pivano might not have discussed the most poorly received work of his career with Hemingway, but it did not stop her from criticizing its inspiration, her rival for his attention. She wrote, without making it clear if she was actually present: 'He often saw Adriana Ivancich, especially at Harry's Bar with two of her friends, and he used to gaze dreamily into her large, bewitching eyes, and take in her curvaceous bust and long slim legs; she was aware and proud of the famous writer's admiration and sat in posed cinema-like positions on the sofa, so as to show herself off to best effect. She would exchange glances with the writer, placing a hand beneath her chin and leaning forwards a little and then giving in to adolescent giggles in an aside to her friend. Hemingway was quite literally lost in gazing at her.'

Later, when Hemingway was back in Italy after having survived two plane crashes and a bush fire in Africa, and recuperating for almost a month in his suite at the Gritti Palace, Pivano remembered: 'His face was emaciated, his hands nearly transparent and without energy, the body broken by his inner injuries and fractured bones. But he did not yet renounce the fight for life. He did not want pictures taken of him. "You should not photograph a beaten man," he said.'

In her accounts of her relationship with Hemingway, she did what she could to maximize its significance, even if neither of the two most serious of Hemingway's American biographers afforded her so much as a footnote in their accounts of his life.

The sudden death of Sottsass's father, in 1953, apparently in robust good health, came as a profound shock to his son. It was an entirely unexpected tragedy. Sottsass senior collapsed on the bathroom floor and was dead twelve days later. Years later Sottsass was still grieving, writing a tribute to his father:

> With his right hand, my father drew countless lines, angles,
> circles and diagonals using all kinds of pencils, rulers and
> glossy black inks; with watercolours he painted perspectives
> of entire cities, buildings and graves; he spent long hours
> erasing failed projects; he measured heights, widths and
> thicknesses; he shook hands with friends and enemies alike,
> with happy people and nervous people, presumptuous

people, frightened people and unhappy people; he caressed my mother's hair and even mine to comfort me when I was a child; he hammered nails and screwed screws; he opened bottles of wine and mineral water; he did up his skis on the memorable day he skied the thirty kilometres cross-country race and, at 4 o'clock in the afternoon on 5 October 1953, he signalled me weakly to come closer when he knew it was time to say goodbye.

His father's death brought Sottsass's first career as an architect to an end. Not all the building projects he worked on in that period had been carried out jointly, but it would be many years before Sottsass returned to a substantial architectural project. Instead, he began to focus more and more on the world of design. What really galvanized the next stage of his career was the chance of spending time in America. Pivano had the offer of a travel scholarship to meet American writers. She was granted a Leader's Fellowship that paid a small daily wage plus travel expenses. At her suggestion, Sottsass applied for the same grant, but was turned down. Late in 1954, Lisa Ponti, at that time managing editor at *Domus*, introduced Sottsass and Pivano to George Nelson.

Though Nelson had trained as an architect at Yale, he had become much better known for his role as an industrial designer and creative director. Almost a decade older than Sottsass, Nelson knew enough Italian to strike up an immediate friendship with him that would endure until Nelson's death thirty years later. After he graduated in 1931, Nelson won a two-year scholarship to the American School in Rome. He set off to interview a number of leading architects, including Mies van der Rohe and Le Corbusier, conversations that triggered his early career as a journalist. He met Gio Ponti, as well as Marcello Piacentini and Giuseppe Vaccaro. After the war he became the design director for Herman Miller — where he commissioned Charles and Ray Eames to design landmarks of post-war furniture. Sottsass had already written for *Domus*, both about the Eameses, whom he rather impressively described as 'designing a way of sitting, rather than designing chairs,' and about Nelson's own work on lighting.

Nelson was impressed enough by Sottsass to offer him a temporary job in New York at the rate of what Sottsass claimed was the princely sum of US$35 a week. Nelson remembers it as US$125, but both of them recollect that the Internal Revenue Service took a big slice. Nelson's Lower East Side office on Park Avenue South was to be a model for Sottsass's own studio. It combined graphic design, architecture, furniture and product design. Unlike the tiny Italian studios that existed entirely to serve their founders, Nelson employed a range of individuals who made their own distinct contributions. Arthur Drexler worked there for a while before he moved to the Museum of Modern Art as chief curator of the department of architecture and design.

Sottsass and Pivano crossed the Atlantic to New York in a silver-hulled TWA Super Constellation aeroplane that took off from Rome on 6 March 1956 with refuelling stops in Ireland and Newfoundland. It was the same week that the *New York Times* announced the start of construction of Mies van der Rohe's Seagram Building. Gordon Bunshaft's Lever House had been finished a couple of years earlier, just across Park Avenue from the Seagram site. It was the high point of American Modernism, a movement apparently on the brink of delivering a glassy utopia. America was a place that offered, to European eyes, unheard of novelties on every scale, from skyscrapers to colour photography. Just five years later the Pan Am Building would, at the urging of Marcel Breuer, close the view of Park Avenue, and bring the brief moment of an endlessly optimistic belief in shiny new modernity to an end.

However, at the moment of Sottsass's arrival, America's future still looked intoxicatingly positive. 'Today, wherever you go, you are jaded, you have seen it all before in the movies or on TV. But there was still no TV in Italy then, I certainly had no TV, and in any case there were no programmes I knew about American architecture; it really did look just like *Metropolis*, everybody running around, nobody caring.'

As soon as they arrived, Pivano set off on a tour of American Ivy League campuses, while Sottsass started work in Nelson's studio. Sottsass, in his self-deprecating way, suggested that he did little more than hang around the office and go sightseeing. 'George Nelson had things of his own to do, the other guys at the studio were busy [...] I wandered around aimlessly like a character in a movie by Luis Trenker; a Bolzano filmmaker in which a character from the Tyrol, a poor devil, ventures into town, looks at the shop windows, some with chickens in them and then goes home, because he hasn't made it.'

Sottsass remembered the warm fluorescent lights at Nelson's office. And the downlighters in his apartment; light coming down from holes in the ceiling. 'You couldn't see the bulbs but you could see the light. And there was the odour of fitted carpet and of paints that I had never experienced before. Just as I hadn't seen the colours, certain bright orange colours and certain blacks.'

Sottsass portrayed himself as a star-struck provincial lost in New York. In fact he was doing his best to make the connections he needed for his future, and Nelson did all that he could to help. Sottsass took a selection of his drawings with him. He called them 'agglomerations of signs crossed by lines, or chessboard patterns'. He claimed that they horrified the then director of the Whitney, 'because there was too much contrast between one thing and another'. It was an introduction that was presumably made through Nelson. Sottsass's account is unlikely to reflect what actually transpired in 1956 with the Whitney's director, an American artist by the name of Hermon More.

Sottsass did succeed in persuading Betty Parsons, the pioneering 57th Street gallerist who worked with Jackson Pollock, Mark Rothko, Ellsworth Kelly and Robert Rauschenberg among many others, to take some of his drawings. She came to Italy the following year to see him. Some of those drawings were much later offered for sale by a collector in Los Angeles.

The Nelson team was working on the famous Marshmallow sofa, which would be launched by Herman Miller that same year. They were also designing an office for the president of CBS in the company's newly completed office tower built by Eero Saarinen and working on the Executive Office Group that made open-plan office life possible. Gordon Chadwick was leading the team building a new factory that Nelson's office had designed for Herman Miller in Grand Rapids. And the office was continuing to develop the Experimental House Project, a speculative look at the future of the domestic world that clearly fascinated Sottsass. It was an interior made up of interconnected modular pavilions topped by Perspex bubbles, motifs that would soon appear in Sottsass's own work. This was the summit of mid-century modernity, in its American version, shorn of the utopianism of Europe, relying instead on the lush sensations of newness.

Almost thirty years later, Nelson wrote an account of the New York launch of the Memphis collection for the April 1983 issue of *Interior Design*, in which he recalled the time that Sottsass had spent in his office in 1956:

Ettore Sottsass Jr was in a large apartment next to the exhibition gallery, having a late dinner with friends, disciples and the gallery owner. He is the only European I have ever known who is a 'Junior', but no doubt there are others.

Years ago, before Castro took Cuba away from us, Sottsass and his wife came to New York. To pass the time, he took a job in my office, where we worked together on a stillborn project called the Experimental House.

The office paid him $125 per week, not a generous stipend even in those far off days, and, to add insult to injury, the IRS had insisted that this unregistered foreigner kick in $30 every week towards income tax. Our problem in the office was that there was no client for the Experimental House, but even so, while we had a good time together, Ettore never got over this example of parsimoniousness. When I got to the gallery and went next door to the apartment, he introduced me to everyone, and then promptly told them the story about the miserable $125 per week and the outrageous $30 so callously levied by the IRS. All the young Memphises looked up from their dinners, turning their large liquid eyes reproachfully at me, as if I had been the IRS and murmured sympathetically in the direction of their guru.

Nelson's connection with Herman Miller had shown how contemporary design could transform the reputation of an established but fading American manufacturer. Other firms were keen to follow the example they had set and hired Nelson to repeat the process. Irving Harper, one of Nelson's long-term associates was responsible for glassware made by Morgantown Glass and cutlery for Chas Bridell. The year 1956 also saw the completion of a house in the Hamptons commissioned from Nelson by Otto Spaeth, an art collector and a board member at the Whitney Museum who presumably opened the door to its director Hermon More.

A couple of weeks after his arrival in America, Sottsass met Pivano in Miami. They were on their way to Havana, to see the Hemingways for a fortnight's stay at their *finca*, with its white tower and its art collection of Klee, Braque and Gris hanging on the walls of the living room in the brutal sun. Hemingway was in a troubled state when his guests arrived. He couldn't finish the book about his African experiences that he was working on and instead cranked out a stream of short stories and magazine articles. Yet Sottsass remembered being embraced by the Homeric Hemingway, his chest full of white hair. He photographed Hemingway in bars, boats and at home with his cat. Sottsass went back to New York by way of Haiti and Puerto Rico.

These few months in America transformed Sottsass. On a practical level, the trip introduced him to a number of people that would prove important for his career. Nelson himself, of course, but also Nelson's friends. Irving Richards, who owned Raymor (otherwise known as Richards Morgenthau & Co) a business on Fifth Avenue, was particularly significant. Raymor was a company that played an important part in popularizing Modernism for American consumers. Richards imported European products, but also did some manufacturing on his own account. He bought some of Sottsass's textile designs. Richards saw Sottsass again in Europe. He paid his hotel bills on the trip to Florence, during which he introduced him to Aldo Londi, the art director of Bitossi the ceramics manufacturer. Londi had designed the Rimini Blu range of ceramics, which sold well for Raymor in the US. Londi commissioned Sottsass to produce designs to be handmade by Bitossi's craftsmen alongside those of Piero Fornasetti.

Nelson, who had been associated with the sharpest American architecture magazine, *Architectural Forum*, encouraged a publisher friend to establish a new magazine, *Industrial Design,* in 1954. Nelson introduced Sottsass to the editors, who included the architect Jane Thompson. Sottsass's archive includes layout sheets for the magazine.

New York was as important for what it taught Sottsass about the nature of design, as for the practical connections that he made there.

> I watched George. He moved about day after day, like a man who knows how complicated it is to imagine the future, how complicated it is to design metaphors, with at least a vestige of reliability.
>
> George reminded me of those workers who dig a hole in the ground, and dig very, very slowly, because the hole is very big and deep and they mustn't get tired too quickly. Those workers lift the earth slowly to get to the bottom where there is something to be repaired. Maybe a waterpipe.
>
> George received his slightly aggressive, slightly coarse clients in a hurry to get down to business. And explained things in his hoarse voice and with his measured gestures, enveloped by the holy cloud of his cigarettes. He would explain slowly, as if what he was saying was only just the very outermost tip of a vast iceberg of knowledge,

experience and possibilities, of visions that lay underneath everything that was being said.

You had to say very little to George because that very little was exactly the right possible and sufficient amount. To vulgarize a vision so sophisticated, ambiguous and frail that beyond those few words, it could not have been vulgarized. In over explaining, there is always the risk of denying mysteries, of slowing down the tempo, of stifling the vibrations, and excluding the unknown.

Sottsass went back to Europe aware that American Modernism was different from the Bauhaus variety, that production was not only a practical phenomenon, but also cultural, and that design had to take production into account. Sottsass's time in New York was vital. It was an experience that he later suggested would soon give him a certain credibility with Adriano and Roberto Olivetti, the two most important clients that he ever had. 'For them, I was the man who went to America.'

Olivetti
to
Apple

121

Ettore Sottsass had several versions of the story of how he first came to meet Roberto Olivetti. Roberto was the grandson of Camillo Olivetti, the founder of what, for much of the twentieth century, was Italy's most successful multinational company. Roberto's father was Adriano Olivetti, a hyperactive polymath with parallel careers in politics, technology, business, urbanism and publishing. He was an even more remarkable man than Camillo, although perhaps no easier to live with. Roberto was the last member of the family to have a real part in running the company, but by then the business was already in a financial and managerial crisis. It managed to recover for a while before finally evaporating in a reverse takeover of Telecom Italia, which saw Olivetti take on US$16 billion of debt in a somewhat murky financial transaction and then disappear from the stock exchange.

It was Adriano Olivetti who took the decision to hire Ettore Sottsass, but Sottsass's relationship with Roberto was a personal one. Working with Roberto was the pivotal event of his career. Before they met, Sottsass was unsure about his future. When he made the connection, things became clearer and he became much more confident with his direction in life. After Roberto's death Sottsass drew away from the company. Writing in 1980, Sottsass looked back on his state of mind before he worked for Olivetti:

> After the war, at the age of thirty, I found myself in a country destroyed by violence and conflict, but all the same I was full of hope. But I didn't know what I was going to do. Above all I didn't have a single lira. And not to have a lira was a problem.
>
> I didn't want to teach, because I didn't think I had anything to teach. I saw myself as somebody who still had everything to prove. I couldn't work for myself as an architect because the liberal profession of architecture is a luxury career. It's a career for intellectuals to whom the bourgeoisie only pays on account. The minimum

requirement is a little money to invest in draughtsmen and a studio with a telephone, a secretary and a car. All that I had then was a bicycle. I didn't want to work in the office of another architect — not even that of my father, or in a government studio, because I felt myself to be an artisan, perhaps a somewhat old-fashioned destiny. I wanted to be an artisan, which is to work for yourself, and to think about design for yourself, to build the project, and at the end to be paid for having done the work. For all these reasons and certain others, too many to explain here, I have spent a provisional life, making a little money here and there, with temporary solutions. Sometimes I had money, sometimes not, sometimes I was happy, and sometimes I was desperate. Sometimes I thought I was a great talent, sometimes I thought I was a total idiot.

Olivetti offered Sottsass the most remarkable industrial project of his life, the chance to work on a mainframe computer. At the time it would have seemed almost as extraordinary an idea as working on the first jet engine or the first atomic bomb. As well as Roberto Olivetti, Sottsass made another close friend through the company, Mario Tchou, the engineer leading the electronics programme. Both are among the faces on Sottsass's lithograph of the scribbled-out death masks that he made in 1999. Tchou was thirty-six when he died in 1961. Roberto Olivetti died in 1985 aged only fifty-seven. The connection with the Olivetti family had transformed Sottsass's career; it gave him financial security, it made him famous — and it saved his life.

Adriano Olivetti was born in the modest provincial town of Ivrea, a little north of Turin. By the time Sottsass started to work there fifty years later, the company had grown from a single workshop into an industrial giant with factories in Mexico, Argentina, Spain, Brazil, Scotland and the US. His father Camillo had the idea of making the first typewriters and adding machines in Italy, but it was Adriano who turned Olivetti into a global company, one that set a new model for how a modern corporation could present itself to the world.

Adriano was a resolute anti-fascist and his political convictions made him leave Italy more than once. He spent six months touring American factories during Mussolini's rise to power. His friendship with Filippo Turati, the poet and co-founder of the Italian Socialist Party, would force him to leave the country again. Following the kidnap and murder of his fellow socialist Giacomo Matteotti in 1924, Turati escaped to France with Adriano's help, who then went into temporary exile in London himself.

When his father stepped down from the management of the company on reaching his seventieth birthday in 1938, Adriano became the chairman. Despite the laws that excluded Italian Jews from public life and pressure on Mussolini from Hitler to adopt his anti-Semitic policies, Olivetti was too big and too important a company to be confiscated by the fascists. Adriano, who by this time was listed as a potential subversive by the government, maintained a political silence in public. He had to protect the jobs of his workforce. To this end, it is said, he acquired a Fascist Party membership card. But even before the armistice with the western Allies, Adriano had made contact with the American and British intelligence services and was working on plans for an anti-fascist coup. He was imprisoned for several weeks in Rome for these supposedly treasonable contacts. The German occupation forces threatened the already ailing Camillo Olivetti. He left Ivrea and died shortly afterwards in nearby Biella. Thousands of his workers defied threats and filed past his grave in the Jewish cemetery there.

Adriano was fortunate enough to have been released from prison before the Germans could find him and went into exile in Switzerland until May 1945. Among the other Italian refugees that he met there was Luigi Einaudi, father of Fernanda Pivano's publisher, Giulio Einaudi and soon to become president of the Italian republic.

On his return to Italy, Adriano supported, and sometimes created, the cultural and political institutions needed to underpin a democratic society in the moral vacuum left by fascism. He funded a news magazine and a publishing house, and provided financial support to sociologists and novelists. He even started a political party which, although it saw him elected briefly as mayor of Ivrea, failed to change the balance of power in the Italian parliament.

Even before the war, Adriano had hired talented designers and artists to work alongside his engineers in order to make Olivetti's typewriters seem culturally desirable as well as technically ingenious. In 1940 the company unveiled the MC 4S Summa adding machine that Marcello Nizzoli had styled. As the company grew, Adriano commissioned a number of bright young architects such as Luigi Figini and Gino Pollini whose work he had seen at the Milan Triennale. He asked them to design new factories, to build homes for the company's workers, and to give Ivrea all that a modern town centre needed:

schools, a cinema, parks, a crèche, sports amenities and shops. Adriano didn't limit his vision to his own company. He sponsored a plan for an ambitious regional strategy for the whole of the val d'Aosta area, to show how growth could be planned and infrastructure best be channelled towards the most productive projects.

In 1937 he started his own magazine, *Comunità*, dedicated to exploring his vision of a world in which workers and management shared in the benefits of their labour. Adriano invited Le Corbusier to Ivrea in the 1930s but it was not until after the war that he was commissioned to design an electronics factory the company was planning to build but never realized, on a huge site at Rho, alongside the *autostrada* from Milan to Turin.

After the war Nizzoli was responsible for the design of the Lettera 22 portable typewriter, Olivetti's most charismatic product at the time. The gifted graphic artist Giovanni Pintori started work for the company at the same time as Nizzoli and produced, among much else, a series of elegant and witty posters promoting the new typewriters. Nizzoli remained responsible for the look of most Olivetti products, but Adriano selected a number of new architects to build Olivetti showrooms around the world during the 1950s. Carlo Scarpa designed one of them in Venice, providing an exquisite setting in Piazza San Marco for the company's adding machines and typewriters.

Franco Albini and Franca Helg designed the Paris equivalent. Most striking of all was Olivetti's New York showroom on Fifth Avenue by BBPR, the architectural partnership formed by Gianluigi Banfi, Lodovico Barbiano di Belgiojoso, Enrico Peressutti and Ernesto Rogers. So striking, in fact, that it stopped Thomas Watson, then president of IBM, in his tracks. He was lost for a moment in wonder at the sight of an undulating marble landscape that supported a few exquisite looking machines, and a typewriter impaled on a plinth on the street outside the shop window that gave passers-by the chance to test it at any time. 'Why aren't we as good as this?' Watson asked, and sent his managers to look closely at what Olivetti had achieved and consider what could be done to match their approach. It was a moment that transformed IBM's view of what it could become.

Adriano was determined to keep his company ahead of his competitors in both technical innovation and also in cultural terms. Its expertise was entirely in mechanical systems. If Olivetti was going to survive it had to make a huge leap — embrace electronics or face oblivion. The nuclear physicist and Nobel Laureate Enrico Fermi came to Ivrea in 1949 and talked to Adriano and

Roberto about the impact that the new computers would have on the company and the economy as a whole as they emerged from the laboratories that had developed them. Olivetti opened a research base in the US at New Canaan, in Connecticut, overseen by Adriano's brother Dino. Yet Adriano quickly realized it wasn't going to be enough and he started Olivetti's own electronics laboratory at Ivrea, setting out to find the best possible engineer to lead it.

Mario Tchou, a twenty-nine-year-old Italian born of Chinese diplomat parents in Rome, then working as an assistant professor at Columbia University, was recommended to him. Adriano went to New York to meet him and was impressed. 'He is a man who is seriously interested in people, in social experiments, in the relationship between management and workers, but above all is one of the few who has studied the operation of electronic computers.' Tchou accepted Adriano's offer to work for Olivetti, and by the end of 1954 he was in Ivrea. Adriano gave him the budget to recruit his own staff from around the world. Tchou brought in researchers from England (where the engineering firm Ferranti had already built a mainframe that the Olivetti team bought and took apart), Holland and Canada as well as many Italians. They were all very young. 'Only the young would pitch in with enough enthusiasm,' Tchou said.

Fermi brokered a partnership between his old university in Pisa, which had money to invest in a computer research programme, and Olivetti. Tchou moved to Pisa and established a laboratory with his team in the city's Barbaricina quarter. Adriano made a public announcement at Christmas 1954 that Olivetti would build a computer. Adriano was conscious of the negative impact that the decision might have on the morale of a company dominated by mechanical engineers, and tried, not entirely with success, to sound reassuring. 'Just as the development of the aviation industry has not stopped the production of the car, so the computer will not replace, for the time being at least, calculators and mechanical adding machines,' he told his workers.

The researchers worked in a villa with views across Tuscan vineyards and orchards. Tchou's collaborative management style got the best out of the team. He had a shrewd political understanding of the need to protect his team from suspicious engineers at Ivrea, but also how important it would be to make their work useful to the rest of the company. Whilst developing what would become the Elea, they also designed electronic products that the mechanical division would need.

In his seven-year career at Olivetti, Tchou oversaw the development of four generations of computers. Machine Zero, the first working prototype, later designated the Elea 9001, was completed at Barbaricina in spring 1957. The name said a lot about how the company saw itself. 'Elea' was not only an acronym for Elaboratore Elettronico Aritmetico, but also a reference to the ancient Greek city-state on the Italian mainland with its own school of pre-Socratic philosophy. This first machine was valve driven, large and formless (since nobody had yet thought about its appearance), but Adriano and Roberto gave it the green light. Machine Zero was dismantled and sent to Ivrea to be put back together for use in the company's logistics department.

Having proved the concept, Tchou built a second machine, the Elea 9002, which was also valve driven, but with some transistorized components for data input. It was more reliable and less demanding in its need for sterile conditions and climate control. However, at a Sunday afternoon meeting in the autumn of 1957, Adriano, Roberto and Tchou decided that hobbling transistors with valves was an unacceptable compromise. Even though it would mean a delay of another year before the Elea could reach the market, taking the time to develop an all-transistor machine was a better strategy than rushing out a flawed model destined for instant obsolescence. The hybrid prototype was shipped to Milan for use in Olivetti's via Clerici HQ, and work started on the all-transistor Elea 9003.

Tchou hired mathematicians to start thinking about what would eventually come to be known as software and to create new programming languages that could handle more than pure calculations. He and Roberto set up a semiconductor production plant in partnership with the telecommunications company, Telettra. Tchou and Roberto resisted Adriano's plan to build the next Elea in Ivrea. Not only was Ivrea dominated by mechanical engineers, it was considered too provincial a setting to attract an international workforce. Borgolombardo on the edge of Milan was chosen instead. There they had room to create the Elea, as well as a production line to build it on a commercial scale, in a factory that eventually employed 1,000 people.

While Tchou lead the technical development of the project, Adriano and Roberto began to think about what the new computer should look like. It needed the right designer to give it form and character, somebody who could make it simple to maintain, to install and use, but also somebody who could design a computer that was clearly an Olivetti.

Adriano recruited Sottsass late in 1957. In *Scritto di Notte*, Sottsass suggests that his first introduction to Olivetti was made through Giorgio Soavi, Adriano's brother-in-law, in Ivrea during the last days of the war. Sottsass provides a persuasively detailed account of an event that probably did not happen in quite the way that he describes it. He was stationed with an Alpini unit not far from the town. One morning he shaved particularly closely and then took the bus into Ivrea for lunch in the belle-époque dining room of the Dora Hotel. It was a high-ceilinged room full of elaborate chandeliers and giant mirrors, regularly patronized by Olivetti's managers, where he found a table of serious-looking civilians talking animatedly. One of them was Soavi, who invited him to join them. This account seems unlikely since Soavi had, like Sottsass, volunteered for the Repubblica Sociale Italiana Army. Unlike Sottsass, he deserted in 1944, and spent the rest of the war in hiding in Milan. Sottsass's suggestion that Soavi may have also introduced him to the very young Roberto Olivetti on that day in Ivrea is even less credible. Roberto could have been no more than seventeen at the time, and his father Adriano had escaped to Switzerland after Camillo's funeral. The Jewish heritage of the Olivetti family meant that the Salò republic was no longer safe for any of them.

Perhaps the lunch in Ivrea in 1945 was a premonition. Maybe it never happened. Maybe it was a lunch that took place long after Sottsass had thrown away his uniform, when Italy was at peace and he found himself back in the same dining room that he had first seen during the war. However, Sottsass later told his assistant, Milco Carboni, that he met Roberto long before he started working for Olivetti. 'I don't remember how I met him, but we spent some afternoons together in a bar on the Piazza Castello. He was a lot younger than me, but he was very smart and interested in listening. Truly he was his father's son, which is to say he was as much a cultural as a business figure.'

There is another version, involving a meeting that took place in a different Turin café. 'I first met Roberto Olivetti, perhaps in 1947 or 1950. I met him, I think, through Giorgio Soavi. We were sitting in one of those cafés in the Piazza San Carlo. He was very calm, quiet and modest. I did not see him again for many years, until Adriano, perhaps at Roberto's urging, asked me to become the designer for the electronics division.'

Pivano suggests that the introduction might have been made in 1950 at the opening of an exhibition in Turin and a dinner afterwards at the Amadeo Grill. She knew Natalia Ginzburg, a writer whose sister was Adriano's first wife. Ginzburg was published by Einaudi and was also Pivano's mentor. Perry King, Sottsass's former collaborator believes that it was indeed Pivano who made the connection for Sottsass and persuaded Roberto Olivetti to see him. But in any case, as early as 1949, Sottsass had already contributed an article to

Comunità which, since Soavi had become editor of the journal in 1948, would suggest that Sottsass had met or at least had contact with Soavi by then.

Sottsass gave Carboni another plausible account of how things might have gone:

> One day, the writer Giorgio Soavi asked me to prepare a book of my work, like the kind of thing that fashion models have, to show Adriano Olivetti. He was looking for a designer for the electronics department that he was setting up. I was competing with Marcello Nizzoli and, I think, Vico Magistretti. I don't remember the others. I told Soavi right away that I had nothing to show, because I had done nothing but some baskets, some lamps and trivia like that. I thought that the four blocks of workers' flats that I had done weren't going to be enough to convince Adriano Olivetti.

Soavi was a poet, a novelist and an editor. Adriano Olivetti, whose sister Lidia Giorgio married in 1950, made him the art director for the company. It was Soavi who oversaw the employment of Milton Glaser and Jean-Michel Folon to make posters for Olivetti. He ran the company's publishing arm and oversaw the production of the annual Olivetti diary, illustrated by artists ranging from Graham Sutherland to Balthus. It was Soavi who worked with the Olivetti family to commission Marco Zanuso to build the Olivetti plant in Argentina, Louis Kahn to work for the company in the US and James Stirling in England. After Soavi's death Sotheby's sold the portrait that Alberto Giacometti had made of him in 1963 for £500,000.

It would certainly have been Soavi who contacted Sottsass on behalf of Adriano and Roberto, just as it was Soavi who commissioned Henri Cartier-Bresson to photograph the town of Pozzuoli when Olivetti built a factory there, and who asked Snowdon to photograph Venice. Soavi's sensibility ensured that when Olivetti published a statement of the Elea's capabilities, it used illustrations from fourteenth-century Sienese wool trading account books. It was not only Sottsass's architectural work, or his writing that interested Adriano, his experience with George Nelson in New York would certainly also have attracted his attention.

Camillo, Adriano and Roberto had all studied in the US. Camillo lectured at Stanford before Silicon Valley was even dreamed of. Adriano bought

Underwood, the American typewriter business (which, at the time, was the largest foreign takeover of an American company) in the hope that it would allow Olivetti to acquire US expertise. America, he believed, was going to achieve more in technical development in the next five years than Italy could manage in twenty-five.

The Underwood acquisition was part of the strategy for reshaping and modernizing Olivetti, though it proved to be a questionable one. The American firm was a long way behind Olivetti in ambition, technology and design. It had been spending its earnings on high dividends for shareholders, rather than investing in research. When its competitors started making machines it could not compete with, it faced a cash crisis — one that Olivetti believed it could solve.

Sottsass was intoxicated with the possibilities of the new project: 'How could we build an entire electronics business from zero? I was forty, Roberto and Mario around thirty. How were we going to make a world inhabited by electronic machines? We shared a utopian vision of enlightened capitalism. We were bourgeois intellectuals, bourgeois but anti-fascist intellectuals, bourgeois of the left.' But even in this apparently benign climate, Sottsass was still anxious about what he was letting himself in for: 'I worried about being sucked into the corridors of power, and squeezed dry like a lemon. I was worried about being neutered.'

So Sottsass became a consultant rather than an employee. Adriano Olivetti had surrounded himself with the most creative and talented people that he could find, paid them handsomely and put them to work on projects that would do justice to their skills. Sottsass's contract allowed him to maintain his own independent studio, and was generous enough to make him financially secure. Sottsass had a team, access to the craft workshops established by Olivetti to work on prototypes and models, and a budget to run. But he was never going to look or act like a conventional manager. He had no intention of turning his performance as Lieutenant Sottsass of the Alpini into a rehearsal for middle management in a typewriter factory.

Nizzoli's work for Olivetti had made him perhaps the best known of Italy's industrial designers. To be appointed to a role that would make him Nizzoli's successor was the clearest possible endorsement of Sottsass's significance as a designer. He had so far had only moderate success as an artist. He had designed stands at trade fairs and museum displays. There were some promising ceramics and metalwork, and one or two interiors that had attracted some attention, a lot of photographs and some book designs. He had started to design domestic furniture for the newly established Poltronova factory in Tuscany. Thanks to Olivetti, however, Sottsass was able to shape a large part of the landscape of the workplace rather than merely to speculate about its nature from the sidelines. Design that touches millions of people usually does not come from the studio of an isolated designer. It emerges from those manufacturers who have the resources to invest in a new product and access to the technical expertise to make it.

Of course Sottsass did not design the circuitry or the transistors, or have an understanding of the coding that made the Elea work. In fact Sottsass was dismissive of a narrow focus on technology. The British designer George Sowden, who worked with Sottsass at Olivetti, remembers that he always mockingly called computer monitors 'televisions'. However Sottsass had the imagination to make a machine come alive, to give it a character that people could engage with. And he achieved that essentially through the closeness of his relationship with Tchou, an exceptionally open-minded scientist, and his continuing ability to connect with Adriano and Roberto.

Sottsass was working on the most critical project in Olivetti's history. It was work that put him at the heart of Italian life. In the first few years of the friendship with Tchou and Roberto there were parties in Sottsass and Pivano's apartment on the via Capuccio in Milan, and then in their much smarter place on the via Manzoni at which Roberto would be in one corner of the room, the writer Alberto Moravia, the artist Arnaldo Pomodoro and the publisher Giangiacomo Feltrinelli in another. Milan was a town full of factions that rubbed each other up the wrong way, but was not large enough for them to be able to avoid socializing together. Sottsass was an ally of Gio Ponti, which meant that he was unlikely to be a friend of Ernesto Rogers. Yet both Rogers and Ponti came to the parties that Sottsass and Pivano hosted. They were one of the best-connected couples in Italy, bringing together a glamorous mix of visiting Americans (including Chet Baker and Jack Kerouac), Italian intellectuals, Swiss artists, filmmakers, bankers, writers and businessmen. There was wine and whisky, vodka and a fair amount of marijuana. Tchou and Sottsass would holiday on Roberto's yacht. They went to New York together and found themselves in Andy Warhol's studio.

Tchou asked Sottsass to design his Milanese apartment for him. Sottsass started to carve out the interior from the fabric of a 1930s building. He created an indoor landscape with terrazzo floors and a sequence of spaces flowing one into another, punctuated by specially made furniture towers that were both totems and practical means of storing books and dividing space. They were made by Sottsass's friend Renzo Brugola, who had worked with him on the furniture that he designed for Poltronova, and would be responsible for making the best of Sottsass's Memphis pieces. Tchou died before the apartment was finished and Sottsass's near fatal illness in 1962 meant that Tchou's widow and her children couldn't move in for another year.

Sottsass's first role at Olivetti was to give the Elea its character and identity. He needed to convey what it was, and how it was to be operated, as well as to give it a practical form. The project gave him the opportunity to explore the emotional as well as the practical aspects of human interaction with computers. They were still very costly and unfamiliar artefacts — and, for the first time, they raised the troubling, even threatening possibility of intelligent machines.

Sottsass worked with Tchou and the other engineers to understand how best to configure the memory banks, which took the form of tangles of knitted ferrite wire, arranged in modular frames to increase capacity, looking like racks of honeycomb in a beehive. In 1955, IBM was just beginning to think about transistorized solid-state computing. The machines that it, and its very few competitors, had sold up to then had been massive valve-driven monsters, weighing in tonnes and generating so much heat that they needed special air-conditioning to function. The message that these machines communicated to their users was not of paramount concern when Alan Turing and his team at Bletchley Park had struggled to decode the Enigma machine using Goliath, the ancestor of all mainframe computing. Bletchley wanted the data outputs to save lives and win a war; everything else was a distraction. The early computers were permanent installations, in which machine and building merged into one. They looked complicated, scientific and makeshift. The first American commercial computers were still monsters that weren't going to move anywhere; but there were attempts at least to make them look neater, to hide their guts away in tidy metal cabinets, as if they were some kind of telephone exchange or unusually elaborate dental equipment. Sottsass wanted to do something different.

He began by stepping back to think about what was at stake. 'What should a computer look like?' he asked in a letter that he wrote to himself. 'Not a lathe, not a piece of furniture, not like a washing machine.' He explored practical issues such as maintenance, access and adaptability. And he also worked on aesthetic and semantic questions: 'What are the things that distinguish an

132

electronic machine from all the other machines? Should these things, if they exist, be emphasized? What parts of the machine should you be able to see all the time, and why?' In the days of unreliable circuitry it needed to be immediately apparent if something went wrong and where to replace defective parts.

On the back of the piece of paper upon which he wrote his letter are a number of pencil drawings in red and blue. They show the bent-rod system that Sottsass devised to carry cables in the simple U-shaped steel frames for the cabinets that contained the spun copper wire at the heart of the system. Further studies, drawn on old stationery from his former Turin address, explore how high to make the computer cabinets.

Sottsass made something of a breakthrough by conceiving of a computer as a collection of individually manageable parts, to be slotted together as needed to build the required capacity. Different users would need different machines. Olivetti could provide them in a series of measured steps and sizes. The Elea had no screen, and a capacity of less than one million alpha-numeric characters (not enough to accommodate a complete Tolstoy novel), in a machine that was twenty metres long and eight metres deep. It sprouted cables at a high level, rather than demanding a raised floor to conceal them as its competitors did. The arrangement made it easier to install, and it suggested that the Elea was a discrete object, rather than an integral part of the building in which it was housed. The Elea wasn't a single monolithic machine, but was made up of a family of separate objects. There was a control unit, equipped with a colourful collection of grids and buttons. There were the memory cabinets formed of hives packed with woven ferrite wire. And there were the data input and output units that ran on paper punch tape spooling in and out of a reader. The units themselves were a mix of colours, and were embellished both with the Olivetti logo and a special branding that Sottsass devised specifically for the Elea based on one of his own drawings; a cluster of black lines that referred to the ferrite wire wrapped inside the memory banks of the machine.

The completed Elea 9003 occupied a space the size of a generously proportioned living room, but it was designed so that its operators, who tended to it in air-conditioned sterility, were not made to feel as if they had been swallowed up by a machine. No component would be higher than 1.5 metres, allowing the crew to see each other. Sottsass combined a feeling for the emotional qualities of design with this sensitivity for the individual. The keyboards and control panels for the Elea 9003 seemed to communicate that you were in touch with something important and momentous. This was the portal to the future, and Sottsass made it look the part by searching his subconscious memory for the visual clues suggested by sacred objects through the ages. He treated the computer as if it were some kind of shrine. Its power was celebrated by its formal design, not concealed by the neutrality of an anonymous container.

In 1986, Sottsass told the writer Gianni Barbacetto in *Design Interface*:

> When I designed Elea, I considered the computer as a
> character, or a personality, that back then scared me
> a little bit. It was a huge, unsettling presence, relegated
> to laboratories. It was not yet a mass phenomenon.
> It was still a presence that aroused suspicion, it was
> intimidating — and in fact I designed it as something
> hidden, behind large aluminium panels, as if it were
> a mysterious deity. Even then, I tried, in my fashion,
> to depict the machine as a cultural statement, not as
> a neutral more-or-less functional mechanism, but as
> a character whose presence affected the lives of those
> with whom it came into contact. Today, I am no longer
> afraid of machines. I am no longer suspicious and when
> I design them, I am still saying something to people
> that goes beyond pure functionality.

The Elea 9003, which could run three programs simultaneously, went onto the market in 1959 — at the same time that Adriano was concluding the deal to take control of Underwood. The Elea 9003 sold, or rather leased, forty units, but only to Italian companies: the Monte dei Paschi di Siena bank, Fiat, La Motta, Lancia and a few others. In 1960, Tchou and his team started working on a simpler, less costly machine, the Elea 6001, aimed at government departments and universities. It did better than the 9003, selling to one hundred users.

The company was beginning to explore the market in Eastern Europe and China. Olivetti had a vision of where the world of technology was moving and the Elea itself was a convincing machine to get it there. However, at the point of the company's heaviest investment in its computer development programme which coincided with the most challenging phase of Olivetti's takeover of Underwood, Adriano died. Sottsass remembered his death vividly. He had presented his designs for the new Tekne electric typewriter to Adriano only a few days before. Adriano, who still felt more comfortable with Nizzoli's aesthetic approach than that of Sottsass, had looked at the models made in exquisite pearwood in silence for some time before leaving the room.

'Mr Adriano Olivetti was a nice man, and super intelligent,' Sottsass told me. 'He made one big mistake... he thought design was about art.' Sottsass had designed the Tekne 3 as an object that — since it would be deployed in dozens, if not hundreds, in a typical office — needed to recede into the background, not impose itself as a work of sculpture. 'He looked at the machine for five minutes without saying a word. "Thank you very much," he said. Then he went away. He phoned me four days later, and told me, "I understand that it is the future of design, but I prefer the idea of design as art. Put a sun on the front, something that will show that it is art, not just technology."'

It is a clash that suggests a side of Sottsass that sits in striking contrast to how his work is now understood. It suggests that Sottsass always pursued multiple strands: he made emotional, expressive work yet was also interested in a cooler, more rational approach. It is notable that Sottsass's first two employees in his team at Olivetti were both graduates of the ultra functionalist Ulm school, and that Tomás Maldonado, also from Ulm school led the research project on which the keyboard for the Tekne 3 was based.

The following week Adriano caught the train from Milan to Lausanne and suffered a fatal heart attack whilst on board. Adriano's death turned out to be only the first of a series of traumas suffered by Olivetti over the next eighteen months.

Roberto was judged by other members of the Olivetti family to be too inexperienced to succeed his father. Giuseppe Pero, the family's long-term consigliere (Pero had taken on the leadership role in 1943 when Adriano was forced to flee to Switzerland), was appointed to take control, but Pero himself fell ill before he could deal with the increasingly obvious problems at Underwood. He was succeeded by industrialist and politician Bruno Visentini who, in turn, was followed by Ottorino Beltrami.

Having lost his father, and with no clear succession in the leadership, Roberto struggled to maintain his vision of the company as an innovator. Sottsass remembered:

> **Roberto had two very difficult simultaneous tasks:**
> **to continue his father's social project and, at the same time,**
> **to move from a mechanical to an electronic culture.**

I remember high-level meetings at which Olivetti and Tchou presented their view of the future to suspicious mechanical engineers. The young industrialist and his young Chinese engineer friend were offering them a journey into the unknown; they thought it was premeditated suicide.

These were engineers who still believed that mechanical adding machines with moving parts, cams, gears and levers could be made intricately and skilfully enough to compete with valves and transistors, and even with the yet-to-be-manufactured silicon microchip.

Then Tchou died in the back seat of the Buick that his chauffeur crashed into a lorry on the *autostrada* to Milan from Turin. Six months after that, Sottsass, who had set off on a protracted tour of India, became so ill that he almost died too. He had been unwell ever since he got back from India in October 1961. After the New Year and Tchou's funeral, he finally went for blood tests. Picking up the results on 10 January, he heard a nurse say, 'This one hasn't got long.' When he told her that they were his, she urged him to go and find the best doctor that he could. None of the specialists he saw could offer anything until Roberto found John Luetscher, the senior consultant at Stanford University's Medical Center, who happened to be in Italy for a medical conference. Luetscher had developed an experimental treatment for Sottsass's condition. A room was booked for Sottsass, who flew to California with Fernanda in May 1962. After many tests, he was prescribed Prednisone, a cortisone-based treatment. He remained very sick, coming close to death and unable to sleep night after night, before the medicine started to work.

The months that Sottsass spent in hospital had a defining impact on him. With Nanda in a chair beside him, they passed the time by producing the *East 128 Chronicle* (the name comes from the number of his hospital room). It was a cyclostyled newsletter to be sent to his friends and looked like the kind of underground magazines that West Coast hippies were producing at the time, full of collages made with advertising images cut from local newspapers as well as Sottsass's own drawings and texts.

By 21 July, he had enough strength to move outside his room. Two weeks later, he checked into a motel in San Francisco where Pivano set him up with a folding table as a kind of temporary studio while he recovered gradually. At the end of September, Sottsass was well enough to go to a baseball game, and then to dinner in Haight-Ashbury, while Pivano was meeting Ferlinghetti and Ginsberg. They finally set off for home via New York in October and arrived back in Milan on 6 November 1962.

They celebrated Sottsass's survival on New Years's Eve in Egypt. According to Pivano, she used a penknife to slice up the two white wristbands that had identified Sottsass in hospital, placed them on a small sacrificial altar in front of the Sphinx, and set fire to them with a match.

While Sottsass was away, unable to work for almost a year, leadership of Olivetti's design effort on the Programma 101 was taken on by Mario Bellini, a discovery of Roberto's who had joined Olivetti at the age of twenty-seven, shortly before Sottsass fell ill. When Sottsass left, Bellini was a junior designer; by the time he returned, he was dismayed to find that Bellini had his own team in place. It was the start of a continuing friction between two very different personalities and an expression of the ideological divide that opened up in Italian design in the 1960s. It was a divide between those who saw themselves as radicals and those that the radicals represented as cultural conservatives, content to play the part of elegant stylists without questioning the basic assumptions of what they were doing.

The under-performance of its American subsidiary and the scale of its investments in new technology in Italy, meant that by 1964 Olivetti was in such serious financial trouble that the company needed a bail-out from a consortium lead by Fiat and Pirelli. A condition of the rescue was that the Elea unit would be sold off to General Electric. Olivetti in the 1960s was still resilient enough, however, not to crumple entirely. Alongside the work on the Elea series, Sottsass had been shaping the Tekne 3 despite Adriano's misgivings, and followed it with the even more successful Praxis 48 electric typewriter. The electronics team had also devised the specifications for the Programma 101, a machine often regarded as the world's first desktop computer. The Programma had been successfully launched in America by the time of the sell-off, attracting a lot of attention, and it remained with Olivetti.

The Elea and the Programma represent technical and philosophical opposites, a moment of evolutionary divergence, of the kind encapsulated by the emergence of Homo sapiens from a boiling gene pool in which it left other varieties of early mankind behind. The Elea was a device intended to operate at the scale of an entire organization, carrying out centralized tasks. The Programma decentralized computing to the individual desk for the first time, and was thus a much more fertile evolutionary prospect. The two machines also represented two very different approaches to design. The Elea's painterly qualities: the multicoloured keyboards and the patterns formed by the grids framing them, reflected Sottsass's very particular sensibilities. Bellini's ability to create smoothly sculpted, perfectly-proportioned industrial objects made the Programma a category-defining object. His rapid emergence as a significant designer in his own right set the scene for Olivetti in the 1960s and 1970s to maintain two parallel design studios in Milan, operating two very different ideologies, and with distinct stylistic assumptions. One was led by Sottsass with a group of assistants that included a variety of nationalities. Perry King and George Sowden were the first of a series of Englishmen to work with him. He hired Hans von Klier, a German born in Czechoslovakia, and Andries van Onck, born in the Netherlands. Masanori Umeda arrived in Milan from Japan in 1970 with a couple of talented Japanese colleagues, the most intriguing of whom was Koichi Tateishi, an artist who came to work for Sottsass's Olivetti studio in 1969 and quickly began to illustrate his most speculative projects.

Mario Bellini's assistants were mostly Italian: Antonio Pio Macchi Cassia, Arnaldo Pasini and Sandro Pasqui amongst others. Sottsass moved studios regularly: from via Cappuccio to the via Borgonuovo, to via Manzoni and then via Melone. In theory, Sottsass and Bellini's studios were assigned different product categories. Bellini worked on desktop projects and Sottsass was supposedly focused on systems, but Sottsass also designed typewriters and calculating machines. It was, however, immediately obvious which team was responsible for which product. Relations between the two remained strained.

Bellini developed a reputation for tactile elegance, exemplified best by his Divisumma 18 electronic calculator, a machine that came in sunshine yellow with a rubber skin that stretched over the electro-mechanical buttons. He once put up a slide of the buttons in profile and followed it with an image of a pert nipple and a finger. The splash of orange plastic on the reels of Sottsass's Valentine typewriter was perhaps a more subtle erotic allusion.

Sottsass's work outside Olivetti, characterized by the candy-striped laminate storage units for Poltronova and his giant-sized ceramic menhirs, was increasingly free. Yet he maintained a rigorous simplicity in the stream of business machines that emerged from his studio, until the Valentine burst into colour, and the Synthesis office chair emerged in shiny yellow plastic with a concertina rubber sleeve for its adjustable column base — both clearly pieces of Pop-inspired design.

The way in which Sottsass was able to recruit gifted young designers demonstrates the key place that his studio at Olivetti had begun to occupy on the global design map, as well as his skills as a talent spotter. Perry King, who was at art school in Birmingham in the 1950s (where he was taught by Naum Slutzky, a Bauhaus veteran), was one of the first from Britain. King was determined to work for Sottsass from the moment he saw a copy of *Stile Industria*, the Italian design magazine that featured the new Elea, in his college library. He wrote to Sottsass in 1964 enclosing some of his drawings, and one or two of the projects he had completed for the Midlands lighting company Best and Lloyd after leaving college. Then he called him on the telephone, and, on receiving a vaguely encouraging reply, immediately set off for Milan.

King — who would go on to work on a wide range of user interfaces for Olivetti with his professional partner Santiago Miranda, before establishing their own design studio — remembers working in the first Sottsass studio in the via Cappuccio, in the same building in which Sottsass lived. He remembers Pivano calling the studio to find out where her husband was, and Sottsass talking about consumerism and new ways of thinking. 'It had a dramatic effect on me,' he said.

King was chosen by Sottsass to work on the Valentine typewriter project. 'He always gave credit to his collaborators,' King recalls. 'There was a discussion in the studio about who should work on the Valentine. "I will give it to King because I can trust him," Sottsass said. He knew that I appreciated what he was trying to do.' The Valentine had 'almost the nature of text messaging,' remembers King:

> We aimed it at young people to have something to
> type with at a cost they could afford. Sottsass proposed
> it to Roberto Olivetti and to Giorgio Zorzi, the head of
> corporate design. As it developed, Sottsass said, 'Put it
> in a bucket you can sit on, and you don't have to find a
> chair.' He wanted to make it only upper case, so that the
> levers to make lower-case letters could be abandoned.
> He really wanted small capitals, but that would have
> meant redesigning the entire mechanism. It was based
> on the existing Lettera 32. Sottsass did not want a bell.

George Sowden was the next British designer to arrive, followed by Charles and Jane Dillon, then by Gerry Taylor and James Irvine. Sowden completed a foundation year at what was then known as Leeds School of Art, before studying architecture in Cheltenham at about the same time as the Rolling Stones' Brian Jones. He left in 1968 and went travelling to the Far East, before he ended up in London working as an architectural draughtsman. He saw a piece about Carnaby Street in Sottsass's travel journal *Memoires di panna montata* ('Whipped Cream Memories') in *Domus*:

> I wrote him a letter, and put some of my drawings in it.
> Sottsass wrote back, 'Come and see me. If you want,
> give me a phone call.' I called from a phone box. He said,
> 'Get a plane; come tomorrow.' When I got to the office
> at via Manzoni, the secretary said, 'He has gone away,'
> 'But he told me to come.' 'You have to wait, maybe
> you wait two weeks. Sottsass told me to give you 10,000
> lire for each day. Here is 200,000.'

Eventually Sottsass returned. Sowden showed him the work that he had done as a student with the vacuum-forming machine that he had built himself, and his prototype chairs. Sottsass hired him and took him to New York where he was working on plans to remodel the Olivetti showroom in a tower on Park Avenue. They went to see Gordon Bunshaft, the building's architect. Sowden remembers:

> As a student, you ask yourself where you get your
> references from. What struck me about Sottsass was
> that he could take references from any place —
> Carnaby Street, things around us, rather than academic
> references. I was instinctively moving to Postmodernism
> and decorated surfaces.
>   The office never closed. Sottsass lived upstairs. At
> that time it was a huge learning process. Every day I woke
> up to something new. He was not a teacher, it was just
> what he had to say. I found it extraordinarily interesting
> stuff. He did not have to say much, I remember at my
> drawing board him saying: 'What are you doing? Don't do
> it like that.' Three days later, 'OK, do it your bloody way.'
>   I was stubborn, as a way of working what I learned
> was to let things happen. When you are a designer,

there is something at the back of your mind, we were doing
machines, furniture, then the other part, the radical,
craft things that are your personal experiments, finding
your own references.

Looking back Sowden sees the years with Sottsass as the glittering last
act of a tradition of industrial culture that was coming to an end:

Olivetti was part of the old world, of real economies
and factories. Its motivation came from engineers,
it was innovative and made the first four-function
mechanical calculator in the word. To copy it you had
to build a factory. Meetings were incredibly important,
there could be thirty or forty people in them, they
had product planners who thought about new things
to do. It was the beginning of the end of the European
factory, end of mechanical culture electronics, and
it coincided with the rise of Postmodernism.

Sottsass gave Sowden the chance to develop his own expertise, which
allowed him to build his career at Olivetti:

In the 1970s there was a lot of noise about ergonomics
and how machines would be used. I looked at it. Then one
day in 1975 Sottsass told me to go to Ivrea. There was a
consortium of Danish banks working on a data centre
and talking about ergonomics. I showed them what I had
been doing. All I had done was put the electronics under
the table. People always looked for the perfect position,
there is no perfect position for the screen, you should just
be able to move it around.

Coincidence was always part of Sottsass's life. Olivetti built its first
computer in 1958. Less than twenty years later, Steve Jobs and Steve Wozniak
produced the first Apple computer in a garage at 770 Welch Road, two miles
from the Stanford University Medical Center in Palo Alto, where Sottsass had
spent those months in a hospital bed. And it was here too that Sottsass was to

design a house for David Kelley, founder of the IDEO design consultancy, in the 1990s. The commission involved demolishing an existing house that had once belonged to John Sculley — the man Steve Jobs brought in from PepsiCo to run Apple, and who subsequently ousted him.

There are striking parallels between Olivetti and Apple's use of design to give their products a seductive quality; both persuade consumers that they are purchasing a desirable artefact that will bestow credibility on them. The Valentine was Olivetti's leap into the world of consumer culture and fashion, using a vivid colour palette to transform business equipment into the expression of freedom. Thirty years later, Apple did the same with the iMac and Jonathan Ive's citrus colour palette. Olivetti built exquisite city centre showrooms. Apple became a retailer. Camillo Olivetti drew the company's first logo himself. Steve Jobs was fascinated by calligraphy and typography. Olivetti hired Milton Glaser and Tim Street-Porter to make advertisements for the Valentine. Jobs spent a fortune on Ridley Scott to film the 1984 'Big Brother' TV commercial for the first Macintosh.

However, the design processes of the two companies, and the cultural assumptions surrounding them, are very different. Olivetti almost from the beginning was guided by the intelligence of Adriano and Soavi in selecting designers. Adriano did not work alone; he trusted the judgement of others and worked with a series of gifted and far-from-obvious architects, designers and artists. In the early days of Apple, Steve Jobs used a seemingly random range of outside designers — from frog design to IDEO, in a range of approaches, mostly in the prevailing beige idiom of the 1980s. The genius of the company was in its intelligent approach to the way in which people interacted with its products. It was only much later, when Jonathan Ive arrived in California, that the ambition to produce computers that were intuitive to use, developed into making them feel equally engaging to touch and to look at.

The difference between the design studios of the two companies in their prime could not be more obvious. 1 Infinite Loop, Apple's address in Cupertino, carries the unmistakable flavour of the vanilla-coloured blocks of a generic high-tech business park, lost in the endless parking lots and lawns hissing with sprinklers that characterize the workplaces of northern California. They are the appropriately bland expression of the kind of lurking, mildly sinister, late capitalism that could have come from the pages of a J. G. Ballard novel. A world corralled behind invisible fences, constantly swept by gyrating security cameras, which has turned its back on the complexities and the random accidents of city life. By 2017, the new Apple building, designed by Norman Foster in the form of a continuous ring and accommodating 16,000 people, will be complete.

Inside the current Apple compound, Jonathan Ive's studio with its butcher-block tables and prototype workshops full of mysterious objects sitting on trolleys, shrouded like cadavers, is a special place, in which a series of remarkable things have been created. However, although Ive can work on charity projects such as a limited edition Leica camera, there is not much else he can do without his employer's approval.

In the 1980s Olivetti maintained two external studios, one for Bellini and his team, the other for Sottsass and his. They were in the same building on the Corso Venezia in the centre of Milan. To reach them, visitors had to pass through a baroque gateway six metres high built from honey-coloured stone in 1652 by Francesco Maria Richini as the entrance to Milan's Seminario Maggiore. It has an elaborate pediment and cornice, and rusticated base, and is flanked by a pair of caryatids. Across the courtyard there was still a chapel on the ground floor of the old seminary building, but the archdiocese had rented out the upper two floors. Mario Bellini's personal studio was under the roof; with life size, black-and-white photographic versions of Gentile Bellini paintings. The first floor was the Olivetti studio; you came out of the lift and turned left for Sottsass and right for Bellini. In those days, Sottsass had his personal studio in via Borgonuovo. Neither he nor Bellini could work for direct competitors to Olivetti, but otherwise they were free to run their own independent studios.

Sottsass was introduced to Jobs by David Kelley. There was a meeting in Milan in Sottsass's studio in the via Borgonuovo. The fastidious Sottsass, by this time out of his radical polo neck and peace symbol necklace phase and wearing an immaculately well-cut suit, did not take to Jobs. Sottsass agreed to put together some ideas about how the studio could work for Apple. However, when Sottsass later visited Cupertino to show his ideas to Jobs, the meeting didn't go well. Jobs, who was wearing shorts and Birkenstock sandals, came down from his office, put his feet up on the glass-top table between them and allowed Sottsass a few minutes to make his presentation in the lobby. He cut the conversation short and got up to leave, but not before handing Sottsass an Apple-inscribed pen as a thank you.

Sottsass's Associati did work later on a portable computer for Apple in the era of John Sculley during the interregnum after Jobs's expulsion. Sculley asked Sottsass to compete with frog design to produce a concept for a laptop.

They produced three alternatives for a prototype for something called the Apple Figaro that never reached production.

Olivetti understood that design is essentially dependent on cross-fertilization. One could argue that if you leave a designer trapped in 1 Infinite Loop, bound by confidentiality agreements, no matter how gifted they are, eventually you will bleed them dry of ideas — as Sottsass himself had suggested when he refused to become an Olivetti employee.

In the end, an open culture for its designers was not enough to save Olivetti and make the jump from the mechanisms of typewriters and adding machines into the age of silicon. Olivetti was once a company regarded as just as vital to contemporary culture as Apple, one that could delight consumers, and that presented itself through a remarkably skilful public relations offensive as the personification of contemporary culture. Even though the name still exists as a brand, the Olivetti of which we speak is dead now. It set the path that Kodak faithfully followed. It delisted from the stock market in 2003 and vanished.

James Irvine arrived in Milan from London in 1978, attracted by the prospect of working for what Olivetti had once been. He remembers that Sottsass had his own room in the studio. 'He had a big wall at the back of his desk, two walls in fact. There were always extraordinary things pinned up. Things that he liked, lots of references, lots of photographs of things that he liked.'

Fifteen years later, in 1993, Olivetti was a troubled company. Cash was short. Its consultants were being paid on 180-day terms. It was being squeezed out of the market by Asian competition and the senior management had lost the sense of direction that the family firm had once had. Sottsass had cut his involvement, leaving his protégé Michele De Lucchi struggling to salvage what he could of its design heritage. Sottsass asked Irvine if he wanted to become a partner in his personal studio:

> I was tempted, but it meant leaving Olivetti. I was still
> faithful to Michele, who was trying to save Olivetti; driving
> to and from Ivrea, negotiating projects, dealing with
> horrible politics. Olivetti was a limping dinosaur, which
> Epson, Canon and the rest were tearing to shreds. I thought
> about it, and decided to say no. I wrote a long letter
> to Ettore to explain why. I went to the studio on the via
> Borgonuovo with my letter. 'Is Ettore here?' I asked.

'No, he is in LA. Just leave it on his desk,' his secretary told me. Ettore's table was always beautiful. There were two sets of coloured pencils, not mixed or random. A flower in a vase by Kuramata, a Japanese high-tech pen, a sheet of paper with a drawing of a stadium in Osaka he was working on and a barometer. I picked up the letter again and decided to become a partner.

In its prime, Olivetti had sponsored a European tour of the four horses of San Marco and commissioned Gae Aulenti and Renzo Piano to make an inflatable pavilion for the exhibition. Olivetti changed the way the office looked. Apple changed not only the office, but also the way that we live. Olivetti belonged to an era when a big company was also a big manufacturer with its own factories. Apple began by having its machines made by contractors in California, then in Ireland and now, it goes without saying, in China. It became the perfect post-industrial model of a corporation. And, unlike Olivetti, it was able to flourish not just in one product category, but in another and another. Olivetti went from the typewriter to the adding machine. It tried the personal computer and died in the attempt. Apple went from the Macintosh to the iMac, then the iPod and the iPhone and has not yet stopped reinventing itself.

Sottsass's personal interests, influenced more and more by his travels to India and his growing friendship with Allen Ginsberg and other countercultural figures, opened up a gap between the business-like, if civilized, world of Olivetti in Ivrea and what Sottsass was doing in the outside world. There is an architectural design for a villa he worked on in early 1961 in which the ground plan shows a garden that is designated in Sottsass's handwriting as a plot for the growing of magic mushrooms and marijuana.

Jobs had made his own pilgrimage to India little more than a decade after Sottsass's first visit. It was an experience that marked him too, but he returned driven by a burning ambition to build a business. Sottsass whose own early twenties had been shattered by the brutality of the war in the Balkans, could see another generation at play and was determined to be part of it.

Radical Sottsass

147

Even before his near-death experience in a California hospital in 1962, Sottsass was looking for an approach to architecture and design that was less materialistic than a conventional understanding of functionalism would suggest. His first journey to India was the trigger, but California, and three months of a drug therapy that left him by turns drained and depressed, followed immediately afterwards and forced him to reassess his life and work.

He went to India for the first time in 1961 when Montecatini, a chemical company, asked him to design its stand at a New Delhi trade fair. Afterwards he went travelling around the country. He told Milco Carboni it was the idea of going to a culture with no tradition of monotheism that appealed to him. He was not an easy travelling companion. In the days of silver-nitrate photography, to take several thousand pictures every week was deeply time consuming. This was at the very beginning of the hippy trail period. A seemingly endless stream of young westerners was beginning to swarm over the subcontinent looking for enlightenment.

Once Sottsass and Pivano left the comparative familiarity of their hotel behind, they saw squalor, poverty and leprosy. Adjusting to India's matter-of-fact acceptance of the universal presence of death was the thing they found most difficult to deal with. The load on the back of the scooter, weaving around them as they negotiated the traffic in a taxi, could turn out to be a corpse in a white shroud on the way to a funeral pyre. 'In India death was normal, it was accepted. The more you had to do with death, the less it was a problem, the less you thought about it,' Sottsass wrote. But the sensual impact of a country full of flowers, scent and colour was as powerful a memory.

Sottsass believed that he was already ill from the sickness that almost killed him before he went to India. The cure took him to San Francisco, which, as it turned out, was not just the place where the doctor best able to deal with his illness was based. It was also where he met Allen Ginsberg, the Beat poet who had already absorbed many of the lessons from India that Sottsass was just beginning to learn.

After he was discharged from hospital, Sottsass was still taking massive doses of the newly developed drug Prednisone. He wrote about its side effects, of the continual vomiting, the weight fluctuations and the depression that came with it.

One of Sottsass's first tangible expressions of the encounter with India, and then with Ginsberg, who had given him a book on tantric art by Ajit Mookerjee, was the ceramic collection that he began working on at the Bitossi factory in Tuscany after he got back from his American hospital. The first of the series, 'Ceramiche delle Tenebre' (Darkness ceramics), Sottsass explained, was a memorial to those whose lives had already been lost. In an article in *Domus*, he named the people he wanted it to bear witness to. Among others they included the two soldiers from the Taurinense Division of the Alpini who were killed in Montenegro and his friend Mario Tchou.

His second collection, 'Offering to Shiva', exhibited in a gallery in Florence in 1964, is a more explicit reflection of Sottsass's interest in India. The deity Shiva represents the continuity and connection between destruction and regeneration. Sottsass's 'Offerings' collection was certainly a reflection of his gratitude for being alive and the pleasure that he took in life.

Sottsass went back to America in 1963 and Ginsberg introduced him to Bob Dylan. Sottsass took a photograph of Dylan during a San Francisco concert. Afterwards Dylan asked Ginsberg, 'Who is that guy with the camera?'

In 1967, Ginsberg went from participating in the first Human Be-in, held in San Francisco's Golden Gate Park, to London to read his poetry and to demonstrate in favour of the legalization of marijuana. Then he travelled to Italy, where he spent much of the summer with Pivano and Sottsass, who put him up in their apartment on the via Manzoni. They took him to the Spoleto Festival, where Pivano was on stage to play Ginsberg's harmonium while he read his poetry. A police officer who picked up Pivano's translation of Ginsberg's words was scandalized enough by some of the language to have him arrested for obscenity. Ginsberg was briefly locked up, but Sottsass got him out of jail the same evening. Then they went to the coast near Genoa to stay with Pivano's mother. It was from there that Sottsass drove him down to Portofino to meet Ezra Pound. Sottsass photographed the event, capturing a notably sullen-looking Pound. Pivano and Sottsass were producing their own underground magazine at the time. Ginsberg is on the masthead as *'Direttore irresponsabile'* with Sottsass described as *'Direttore dei Giardini'* ('Head gardener'). Years later, Ginsberg telephoned Sottsass to tell him that he was dying and to say goodbye.

While Sottsass was immersed in the gentle counter-culture of America's West Coast, Europe's hippies were being pushed aside by an increasingly violent political climate. Terrorism in the Italy of the 1970s had a prelude during the late 1960s in the form of relatively benign street protests that turned increasingly vicious. At first, left-wing students were content to pelt women in fur coats and men in dinner jackets with eggs as they arrived at La Scala for an opening night. Then striking workers from the Pirelli factory occupied the Galleria Vittorio Emanuele II shopping arcade, trapping diners in the elegant walnut-wood and mirrored salon of the Savini restaurant when a clutch of waiters in tailcoats and white ties locked the doors against the mob outside.

The Triennale of 1968, directed by the architect Giancarlo de Carlo, was invaded by angry students who began their occupation on 30 May 1968, the opening day. 'Enough of the fascist Triennale,' cried one placard carried by the protestors, while one of the slogans painted on the wall proclaimed, 'Milano = Parigi'. The Milanese occupiers, mostly from the Brera Art Academy and Milan Polytechnic's school of architecture, were determined to have as much excitement as their counterparts in Paris at the Sorbonne and on the Boulevard Saint-Michel. They were joined by some of their teachers, among them the designer Enzo Mari, a life-long communist, and the artist Arnaldo Pomodoro, both of them friends of Sottsass.

Years later Pomodoro explained what he was protesting against:

> After the war, the Triennale had become an international
> reference point for creativity and design. In those days
> it hadn't been a place in which an object was expected to
> be completely commodified. It was understood that design
> could be regarded as a means of communication and of
> understanding. We hadn't expected that design could be
> used in such entirely different ways.
>
> We had reached the point of revulsion; design
> was still being presented as if it were the product of
> research, and utopian invention. But it wasn't that anymore,
> because in the meantime competition between companies
> intent on selling more products regardless of the quality
> had overwhelmed design. The mass production of
> objects triggered the advertising that has destroyed
> the principles of the Triennale.

According to architect Andrea Branzi, Mari was having it both ways. 'He was outside the Triennale with the students, but he also had his work on show inside,' he told me. Giancarlo de Carlo, who had played a leading part in curating the event had given it the theme of 'The Greater Number,' interpreted variously as referring to designing for mass production or as making architecture for a mass society. De Carlo had the courage, at the age of fifty, to push his way into the Triennale building, which was daubed with the hammer-and-sickle and Maoist slogans, to argue with teenage Trotskyites and Situationists who were determined not to trust anyone over the age of thirty, that he was no fascist. With exhibits from every fashionable architect of the time (from Arata Isozaki and Archigram to Aldo Rossi) to a dynamic installation that included a drag racer halfway up the main staircase, a communications satellite and an all-plastic living environment created by Joe Colombo, there was nothing obviously reactionary about the display. Eventually the protestors left, and the police forcibly reopened the exhibition after the leftist slogans were wiped off the walls.

Despite his radicalism as a designer and the political gestures in his work — one issue of Sottsass's magazine *Pianeta Fresco* featured a series of nude portraits of celebrated Italians presented as a peaceful protest against the war in Vietnam — Sottsass was no street-fighting radical or urban guerrilla. He expressed dissent through wit, not through violence.

Sottsass resolved his own crisis in the 1970s more quickly than Italy managed to emerge from the terror of the *'anni di piombo'* (the 'years of lead') that came at the same time. For the country as a whole, it was a kind of collective nervous breakdown. Sottsass's personal crisis was to an extent shaped by Italy's public trauma, but it was the product of his own circumstances.

The real terror in Italy began after a bomb, most likely planted by an extreme right-wing group who called themselves Ordine Nuovo, exploded in the Banca Nazionale dell'Agricoltura in Milan's Piazza Fontana on 12 December 1969. The blast, clearly audible in Sottsass's apartment in the via Manzoni, killed eighteen people and injured eighty-eight others. The police immediately blamed the left and arrested two anarchists who had nothing to do with the bombing, one of whom then died by falling from the fourth-floor window of the police station. The official report suggested that he had tripped, a statement that inspired Dario Fo's bitter political farce *The Accidental Death of an Anarchist*. Violence, from both left and right, escalated. Communist militants murdered fascist students. The police killed left-wing demonstrators, sometimes by mistake, sometimes intentionally. The policeman held to be responsible for the anarchist's defenestration was shot dead. The pace of the violence and the bloodshed quickened until a shocking catharsis came in the form of the kidnapping and murder of ex-Prime Minister Aldo Moro and his bodyguards in 1978.

For more than a decade political violence, police sirens, street fights and demonstrations accompanied by long lines of blue-grey armoured vans full of bored *carabinieri* waiting for action, formed the inescapable backdrop to daily routine throughout Italy. It could not help but define the climate in which Sottsass lived and worked. Before the blast at the bank in the Piazza Fontana, there had been bombs at Milano Centrale railway station and at the Fiera, the sprawling complex of exhibition halls that staged the regular trade fairs in the city. In both places they exploded harmlessly. Nobody really knew if they had been planted by the left or by the right, or by the right pretending to be the left, or even by the right pretending to be the left pretending to be the right. Groups of militants in their thousands, from both left and right, mobilized every weekend in San Babila in Milan's historic centre and fought with iron bars, chains and knives. No doubt they felt ennobled by the causes for which they were prepared to suffer as they went about their ritualized conflicts.

When the affluent middle classes have stopped driving new cars, going to fashionable restaurants or wearing jewellery and smart clothes for fear of being kidnapped, robbed or murdered, there is clearly little point in a designer trying to give expensive consumer goods a seductive gloss. To retain any connection with a sense of relevance in this traumatic period, Sottsass and other designers used their work to ask questions rather than to provide manufacturers with saleable answers. Rather than work on manipulative consumer goods, Sottsass became interested in what a group of younger architects, including Andrea Branzi and his partners at Superstudio, were doing in Florence. Instead of designing actual cities or physical architectural projects, they concentrated on what was called 'paper architecture', in which the drawing itself was the end product of the design process rather than a means of making a building possible. It is a phenomenon that has a long history; in the eighteenth century Piranesi drew buildings that were impossible to realize. The London-based group Archigram made striking images that suggested the existence of cities that could walk. The Italians in the 1960s were less optimistic and drew endless, featureless and apparently random cities that suggested alienation and also a certain anxiety about keeping up with the Anglo-Saxon world. In one of the drawings that Koichi 'Tiger' Tateishi made for Sottsass, he depicted a rusting, broken-down dystopian version of Archigram's walking city.

Alessandro Mendini, an architect who began his career in the architectural office started by Marcello Nizzoli, though they never met, had become the editor of *Casabella* in 1970, and was using the magazine Giuseppe Pagano had once edited to question the role of design in the consumer society that had brought it into being in the first place. Sottsass was one of the group of architects and designers who gathered around the magazine. Mendini reproduced Tiger Tateishi's drawings for Sottsass's 'Planet as Festival' series (a production that falls somewhere between an American underground comic strip and an architectural manifesto) in *Casabella* in 1972. Mendini took the position that there was already too much design in the world. He had elaborated the conceit for at least a decade or so, concluding that designers had no business designing any more, and should restrict themselves to re-designing things that already existed.

Sottsass's interest in radical design came in part from the American counter-culture that he had witnessed at first hand with Ginsberg, and in part as a response to the political turmoil all around him in Milan. Even before that, Sottsass had worked as an artist, showing sculpture, drawings and paintings in galleries, but simultaneously making mainstream industrial design. During Italy's years of crisis, the balance shifted, and the nature of Sottsass's creative speculations grew wilder. He saw himself as an anarchist, but he identified with the pacifism of American hippies, not the violent anger of Italy in the 1970s. He did however have a close relationship with one of the key figures of the Italian ultra left, and it was a relationship that illuminates the confused and contradictory nature of radical Italian politics.

In Italy in the 1960s, to be rich enough to own a yacht was no barrier to becoming a revolutionary. Giangiacomo Feltrinelli — millionaire publisher and friend of Fidel Castro — and his third wife Inge, were as Pivano put it, 'their dear friends'. Feltrinelli and Inge were regularly to be found at the parties that Sottsass and his wife hosted in the apartment on the via Manzoni, into which they moved in 1966. As a young photographer for a German magazine, Inge had spent a week with Hemingway in Cuba three years before Sottsass and Pivano went to the *finca*. There is a well-known photograph that shows Inge flanked by a fully clothed but apparently inebriated Hemingway and his boatman, in her bathing costume, wrapped around the marlin that the two men have just landed.

After Feltrinelli left her in 1968, Inge sheltered the German activist Rudi Dutschke, who had recently survived an assassination attempt in Berlin. She also began a long-term relationship with Sottsass's former collaborator and neighbour on the via Manzoni, the designer and artist Tomás Maldonado. Sottsass remembered summers in the Tuscan resort of Porto Ercole with Roberto Olivetti, Anna Nogara, the film star who became Roberto's second wife, and the Feltrinellis:

> He [Feltrinelli] had a beautiful Swedish yacht built from teak. One afternoon, with a terrifying wind and huge waves that were keeping everybody else on shore, he asked me if I would like to go sailing with him. There was nothing I enjoyed better than sailing, and we would have gone all the way to Cannes if we had been brave enough. But coming back into the harbour at full speed, Feltrinelli couldn't get the motor into reverse, he just kept coming, and it caused a huge commotion, people were shouting from all the windows overlooking the harbour for him to drop his sail. Then at the last minute, just a metre from the harbour bar, he got the engine working. The whole port went silent for a moment, and then the fishermen in their boats started jeering at the rich who smash everything.
>
> Giangiacomo was a bit like that. Like the old aristocrats, like the few decent rich, Feltrinelli liked taking risks. He did not have the pettiness of party functionaries or tradesmen. It was his destiny to treat everything like a game. Then in the end he played for real.

Sottsass photographed a group of people sprawled on the floor at one of his openings at the Galleria Sperone. There is a man in a blue denim jacket, playing the guitar and leaning against a green beanbag. In front of him, giving every impression of having just handed over a joint, is what looks very much like the figure of Feltrinelli. He is lying on the floor, sporting thick glasses, with a receding hairline, a heavy drooping moustache and sideburns that come close to meeting under his chin.

This was a traumatic time for Italy. Two decades of explosive economic growth after 1945 had not healed the political schism of the fall of fascism.

Prosperity was not enough to ease all the social tensions in the country. Italian politics were dominated by the determination of the Italian Communist Party to join the ruling coalition. The split between right and left was so finely balanced that no single party would ever have a majority. Without a coalition, government was impossible. The communists, who in some elections were able to win as many votes as the governing party, were always excluded from power. Against the background of the Cold War, with a Europe divided between Nato and the Warsaw Pact, America feared Italy would be the Trojan horse that allowed communists into government. The Vatican was equally appalled at the idea of organized political atheism and excommunicated every communist it could find. Between them, Washington and the Catholic Church kept the left out of office.

The Italian Communist Party took up what was called 'Eurocommunism' in an effort to make itself respectable enough to be allowed to share power in coalition with Italy's centre-right Christian Democrats. Led from 1972 by Enrico Berlinguer, the party tried to make what was called a historic compromise with the centre right to give the country a period of stability in the midst of the rising wave of terror. Communist tolerance for the conservative positions of the governing party opened up the ground at the fringes of Italian politics for ultra leftism and, from 1970 when the Brigate Rosse (the Red Brigades) was founded by Renato Curcio and Mara Cagol, for terrorists of the left, alongside right-wing neo-fascist terror attacks. What began as political parties trying to challenge the dominance of the Partito Comunista Italiano (PCI) in parliament turned into something else. When they failed to make an impact at the ballot box, groups such as Potere Operaio (Workers' Power) and Lotta Continua (Continuous Struggle) reorganized themselves into terrorist cells.

Years of elaborately staged street fights between left, right and the *carabiniere*, moved seamlessly into kidnapping, bombing and assassinations. The kidnappings began when two Genoese militants seized a factory manager to raise funds and then quickly merged into the repertoire of the criminal underworld. In Italy, kidnapping became so common that for the best part of the decade, the Italian bourgeoisie had their children educated at boarding schools in Switzerland, and bought themselves apartments in London as refuge from the chaos at home. This was a trauma from which the design world was not insulated. Even *Domus*, the magazine with which Sottsass had been involved since the 1940s, had first-hand experience of the kidnappings. Maria Grazia Mazzocchi, younger daughter of *Domus* publisher Gianni Mazzocchi, was seized and held for several days before being released for a ransom after the magazine's literary editor, who knew people, made inquiries about what it would take to secure her release.

And yet the terrorists were not a self-contained isolated group, cut off from the rest of Italy. For some people, terrorism was a part-time activity. Militants would go underground for a while and then surface in the everyday world that passed for normal. Feltrinelli — who had inherited one of Italy's largest fortunes from his banker father and yet joined the PCI at the end of the war — was a particularly extreme example. Feltrinelli took the view that these were times that demanded action if a right-wing *coup d'état* was to be stopped. He had met with Fidel Castro in Cuba and Régis Debray, a friend of Che Guevara, in Bolivia. He was the first to publish Boris Pasternak's *Doctor Zhivago,* having smuggled the manuscript out of the USSR, and had done well by making posters from Alberto Korda's famous photograph of Che Guevara. He also published books on the strategy of the Tupamaros, urban guerrillas from Uruguay, that proved to be an operating manual for Italy's terrorists in the 1970s, as well as detailed accounts of the exploits of the original left-wing resistance movement between 1943 and 1945, that he saw as the forerunner of the group he established to carry on the armed struggle against what he claimed was an imminent coup planned for modern Italy by the right. By this time he had left Inge and married his fourth wife Sibilla Melega, whom he had met in a Milanese nightclub. She was half Feltrinelli's age and became known as the Brigitte Bardot of the ultra left.

On 16 April 1970, Italy's national TV news frequency was taken over by a pirate radio station: 'Attention, this is the Gruppi d'Azione Partigiana [GAP]. A new mass movement of resistance has been born. A workers' revolt against the bosses and against the bosses' state has been born, and the GAP are reconstituted as the partisan brigades; the workers, the students, united until victory.'

At the time of the broadcast Feltrinelli was forty-seven years old. His *nom de guerre* was Osvaldo. He was found dead two years later on 15 March 1972, apparently the victim of his own incompetent attempt to dynamite an electricity pylon outside Milan.

Italy is a country given to both conspiracy and conspiracy theories. Forty years later, there are still suggestions that Feltrinelli's death was not what it seemed. In 2012, the Milanese daily newspaper *Corriere della Sera* published claims that he might have been killed by one or other secret intelligence service.

Feltrinelli certainly financed the GAP's terror campaign before his death. And even if Feltrinelli himself did not, the GAP did indeed kill people. The gravest, but unproven, charge against him personally is that he helped smuggle Mario Rossi and Augusto Neri of the Gruppo XXII Ottobre out of the country to Prague after they had murdered bank messenger Alessandro Floris in a fund-raising robbery that went wrong. The murder was captured in a horrifying set of photographs taken by a witness. Two men on a scooter attempt to snatch the money that Floris was delivering to a bank. He resists, they knock him down. The pillion passenger turns back and shoots Floris with his pistol as he lies on the ground.

Andrea Branzi never met Feltrinelli, but he remembers sitting with Sottsass in the café of the Continental Hotel just across the road from his apartment on the via Manzoni, and Sottsass pointing at the figure of a man hurrying past on the pavement outside: 'Look, that is Feltrinelli, with his cheeks stuffed full of cotton wool trying very hard not to be recognized.'

Feltrinelli was not the only affluent and privileged would-be revolutionary in Milan in the 1960s. Italy's memories of the Repubblica Sociale Italiana ran deep. For anybody over thirty, the war of the partisans was a vivid memory. In those days the rich could still be on the side of armed resistance. In the 1940s both the Agnelli and the Olivetti families had helped to finance the partisans. The state in the war years, such as it was, had had no legitimacy; its authority was based not on a democratic expression of the people's will, but on the violence of the fascists and on the brute force of the occupying German army.

In the 1970s, the dubious connections of some elements of the Italian secret service with the far right, and with a campaign of right-wing terror that included fatal bombings on Milan's streets, on trains and at Bologna station, were enough to persuade the more melodramatic of the leftists, that the Italian coalition governments of the 1970s were no different to the fascist regime of Mussolini's last year. The left targeted the Pirelli and Siemens factories. Cars belonging to managers were burned. Right-wing unionists and unpopular foremen were attacked. In April 1974, Mario Sossi, a judge in Genoa, was kidnapped by the Brigate Rosse. There were prison revolts. A bomb hurled into the middle of an anti-fascist street demonstration in Brescia killed eight people, and another fascist bomb, placed on a train going from Florence to Bologna, killed twelve more. In the same year, the Brigate Rosse shot dead a policeman, and started what they called the strategy of annihilation, intended to terrorize the ruling élite. By 1976, there were five separate groups of Brigate Rosse active between Rome and the Veneto. They killed not only policemen, but also judges, industrialists, academics and journalists, among them Carlo Casalegno, the assistant editor of *La Stampa* murdered in a hail of bullets in 1977.

On 16 March 1978 the veteran Christian Democrat politician Aldo Moro was kidnapped while on his way to parliament in his car. His four police bodyguards and chauffeur were killed on the spot. Moro himself was held captive, whilst his kidnappers attempted to trade his life for the release of a handful of terrorists held in Italian jails.

The real objective was to humiliate the Italian state, a fact that nobody knew better than the PCI, which refused to countenance any kind of negotiation. Their determination meant that Moro's friends in the Christian Democrat Party couldn't deal with the kidnappers either. The stalemate ended eight weeks later when Moro was shot dead, and his body was found dumped in a car, parked midway between the offices of the Communist and the Christian Democrat Parties. It was a terrible price to pay, but any other outcome would have shown the weakness of the Italian state, not just in its inability to protect its leaders, but also in its lack of will.

The killings did not stop at once. There were between twenty and thirty political murders every year until 1980, but the crisis eventually eased. Italy was on the path to a financial recovery, which seemed on course to put the country ahead of Britain in terms of the size of its economy. In the midst of these uncertainties and anxieties, Sottsass, as he approached sixty, had the sense that there might be another generation trying to push its way past him. There were some issues with Olivetti. The more conservative managers at the company did not relish explaining to corporate customers buying teleprinters and adding machines what the man who designed them was doing showing a ceramic object at the Galleria Sperone in Milan called *Monumento di Merda Alla Patria*. Provided you ignored the title, this outsize ceramic sculpture did not look too challenging. In fact it could be understood as colourful, even engaging.

But by 1971, there was no getting around the fact that Sottsass was making objects that were not only called phallic and clitoral diagrams, but looked unmistakably like that. He was making photomontages — one of which juxtaposed an image of a phallic ceramic vase with a black-and-white photograph of a Red Guard people's court, from the days of Mao's China. Another of Sottsass's images confronted the British Prime Minister Harold Wilson with the same object. He took a series of photographs that captured the troubled nature of the times, including one of the slogan '*Viva la P38*', sprayed on the walls of the University of Palermo in reference to the handgun favoured by the Brigate Rosse.

Sottsass's friend and protector Roberto Olivetti was not the only influential voice in the company and others there were less positive about him. Sottsass had abandoned his faintly dandyish style and adopted a uniform of black poloneck sweaters with a peace symbol dangling from the end of a chain on his chest. He had grown his hair to his shoulders. And his marriage was in turmoil.

Andrea Branzi once suggested that the real victims of radical Italian cultural politics were not the middle classes, who he provocatively suggested rather enjoyed the process, but the generation who, like Sottsass, had come to maturity in the years between the end of fascism and May 1968. Branzi suggests that Sottsass found himself the victim of both left and right. 'The workers of the Poltronova factory played the *Internationale* on the shop-floor loudspeakers, and demanded that the management stop manufacturing Ettore's "useless" furniture. And he was beaten up in Milan for having long hair and wearing an Indian chief's feathered headdress.' According to Branzi, Pierre Restany, long-serving art critic at *Domus*, staged a happening in the Galleria to celebrate the anniversary of the birth of the neo-realist movement. It attracted the attention of a mob of young fascists. Sottsass, in his war bonnet, made the mistake of looking at one of the skinheads. He was immediately attacked and left with a black eye.

Sottsass made a note in his diary at around this time:

> Yesterday Renzo Zorzi and Paolo Viti called me aside, and
> in the course of a contorted, hesitant 'political' conversation
> of the kind that you get in industrial organizations, or in
> political parties, gave me to understand that design at
> Olivetti was in need of some refreshment, but according
> to them, not by me, but by somebody else, only that they
> naturally weren't going to say by whom.

Zorzi was the long-standing leader of cultural and design programmes at Olivetti, groomed by Adriano himself to follow Giorgio Soavi, first as the editor and publisher of *Continuitá*, the company's magazine and publishing house, then to lead the company's patronage of architecture, art and design. It was under Zorzi that Olivetti commissioned James Stirling to build its British training centre at Hazelmere, Richard Meier to work for them on the East Coast of the US, and Kenzo Tange to design Olivetti's building in Tokyo. Viti was the man that Zorzi recruited as his successor. Sottsass took violently against him:

If I could read between the lines, they were trying to tell me that this was the time to turn my job over to some brilliant designer prodigy. Paolo Viti, the accountant elevated to the status of an intellectual, was I think, the dark soul who was the inspiration for this manoeuvre. He was the particular friend of the designer prodigy, his wife was the friend of the designer prodigy's wife, and they had enjoyed many pleasant evenings at their pleasant little bourgeois home. I can't even describe it. I pretended not to understand what they were saying [...] But I still had to defend myself in some way. Perhaps I succeeded, but it left a bitter taste. Getting old is horrible enough, to really know when to stop, if that is what it should be, is difficult. To know who and what will succeed you is even more difficult, but having to accept a crude and manipulative imposition from outside is almost unbearable. This sense of time passing, and what is going to happen without me, the sense that hope is being reduced to a biological condition, that time is running out, gave me four or five years of fear and uncertainty until perhaps I started to find a new equilibrium.

Sottsass did not name the designer he suspected was being groomed to replace him, but both Paolo Viti's wife and the wife of Michele De Lucchi were German and had spent a considerable amount of time in each other's company. De Lucchi's wife Sibylle Kicherer had written a book for Olivetti about its corporate design methods at Viti's behest; a coincidence that has led some to believe that it was De Lucchi that Vita wanted Sottsass to make way for. In fact Olivetti's design team politics were complex in the extreme. Bellini's studio was impregnable. George Sowden, who had been working for Olivetti ever since Sottsass had brought him to Milan in 1970, was by this time in command of much of the computing programs for banking that provided the steady income stream that underpinned the company. Perry King was running the corporate design programme. De Lucchi, who had recently begun to work for Olivetti under Sottsass's leadership, was establishing his place in the company.

Neither was Sottsass deeply engaged at Olivetti during those years. His studio kept ticking over. There was the bravura Pop Art side chair that formed part of the Synthesis 45 office furniture range (which looked distinguished, but was a technical failure) and a few adding machines. By comparison, Bellini's side of the Olivetti design studio had never been busier. In truth, Sottsass had lost interest in the everyday world of mass production and he spent most of his time elsewhere. He had other things on his mind.

Eulàlia Grau was still a student in 1970 when at the age of twenty-three she came to Milan from Barcelona to work in Sottsass's studio — one of the continually fluctuating cast of visitors attracted by his reputation. It was a place that drew people who were looking for an approach to design that seemed to offer more than narrowly technical answers to simple commercial questions. Grau, a Catalan nationalist with connections in the anti-Franco underground and a young woman who regarded herself as an artist rather than a designer, was no exception. Her work took the form of political collage. Sottsass's image of his phallic ceramic object juxtaposed with the people's court seems to have been inspired by the same sensibility.

Sottsass wrote of the day that he met her:

> A girl who was not tall, not obviously beautiful, tiny, with
> a small frame. She had a flat, prehistoric face, and black,
> wiry hair. She smiled. She came in and sat down in front
> of me. She went on smiling, without saying anything. I was
> embarrassed. I spoke. She said a few words but didn't
> understand Italian. As she smiled, her moist lips slid over
> her very white teeth. Her eyes were simple: they were
> dark, but those of a woman; even her eyes were ancient.
> In a flash, in the briefest of moments, I was in love.

Over several years, in a protracted agony of indecision, Sottsass understood that he could not be without her, but that he could not leave his wife either. The four or five years of pain that Sottsass describes coincide exactly with the time that he was with Grau, a period in which he was also at his most ready to explore and experiment with projects that often seemed to have little to do with design in the conventional sense. There were utopian and dystopian drawings of ideal communities, or destroyed dreams often made in coloured pencil and ink by Tiger Tateishi, that looked quite different in their techniques and style from anything that Sottsass had previously done or would do again. In the course of long periods away from Milan, he would set up installations in landscapes, suggesting staircases and thresholds marked out by string and wire.

Pivano suggests that Grau, whom she refused ever to mention by name, deliberately provoked the crisis in Sottsass's life at the beginning of 1972. Sottsass does not use Grau's name in his diaries either, though he does mention the first name of her sister. However, he describes his lover in every other detail. She was an artist, she was political. They would spend weekends in Barcelona, at first in her tiny apartment. Then in a room at the Hotel Oriente, behind its ancient darkened shutters looking over Las Ramblas with its palm trees and its kiosks selling caged birds and books. After Grau and Sottsass had become lovers, Pivano implies that the younger woman called to tell her that her husband was having an affair. Pivano describes the anonymous telephone call as being so hurtful that she took off her wedding ring. Pivano wrote that afterwards someone sent her photocopies of Sottsass's letters. The implication is that it was Grau and Pivano claimed that she destroyed them without reading them. Then she writes that Sottsass received a poison-pen letter abusing Pivano.

By this time Sottsass had already taken Grau with him on a visit to Bitossi, the ceramics factory in Tuscany that he was working with. The young girl in the miniskirt in her early twenties, and Sottsass in his late fifties, created something of a scandal. But, in the way of such relationships, Sottsass felt he could not do without Grau. However he also felt he could not live without his wife of twenty-three years. The relationship was kept from her, until the spring of 1972 when Pivano received the anonymous call that caused her to take off her wedding ring.

Sottsass's solution to his dilemma was to tell Pivano that, although they could continue to live together during the week, they would in future be spending their weekends in different cities. He was going to be in Barcelona with Grau. He wanted Pivano out of the way in Rome or Milan. She described it as a farcical situation, but nonetheless she accepted it, distraught though she was. They went on in this way for almost four years. There were many days when the courtyard of the apartment block in which they lived was filled with the sounds of Pivano's anguish. In the 1980s, Pivano published her first novel, *Cos'è più la virtù: Romanzo quasi d'amore*, which described the collapse of a marriage that sounds much like her own. It is a *roman à clef* chronicling the life of a writer, her travels and her love for the husband who leaves her. She asks herself if the real betrayal was his passion for another, younger woman or her wasted fidelity to him as she reflects on all the suitors she rejected over the years.

Alessandro Mendini, with whom Sottsass had a relationship of varying closeness over the years, would sometimes go to Barcelona with Sottsass for one of those weekends. 'He was just like a student,' remembers Mendini. It was an increasingly schizophrenic period for Sottsass. He was travelling more and more; anything to be out of Milan. In his work for Olivetti after the brilliance of the Valentine, he was treading water. But his personal projects were becoming increasingly wild and political.

Seen from close quarters, Italy in the 1970s was a traumatized and unstable place. From further away there was a different story to tell. The outside world was beginning to recognize that Italy, or at least the Italy of Milan and the north, had become the most creatively interesting place in the world of design. Gio Ponti and Ernesto Rogers, the opposite poles of the pre-war generation had built a new city, its skyline marked by the extremes of the sleek, tapered and sculptural Pirelli tower, and the neo-historicist Torre Velasca. Ponti's design work, such as his furniture for Cassina and his cutlery, had become the signifier of contemporary design everywhere, just as it had once been glass from Finland or wooden furniture from Denmark and Sweden.

Ponti and Rogers were followed by a new generation led by Sottsass and slightly younger names: Mario Bellini, Joe Colombo, Vico Magistretti, Achille and Giacomo Castiglioni, Enzo Mari, Gaetano Pesce, Gae Aulenti, Cini Boeri and Anna Castelli Ferrieri. Almost all of them were based in Milan, in a remarkable concentration of creative talent that no other city in the world could match. It was a concentration that began to attract ambitious young designers from all over the world. And there was also the support of modelmakers and craftsmen, as well as a network of specialist manufacturers to commission their work. It produced a self-sustaining critical mass of designers and design talent.

In 1972, the extremely precocious Emilio Ambasz — who at twenty-four was already a curator at New York's Museum of Modern Art — organized 'Italy: The New Domestic Landscape', a sprawling and ambitious exhibition that signalled for perhaps the first time just how much attention the rest of the world was paying to the significance of Italian design. However, while few non-Italians who saw it would have understood, it also demonstrated the deeply polarized situation in which Italian design found itself. In deference to the financial support offered by the Italian ministry of trade, one section was devoted to a collection of all the exquisite and seductive products of Italian factories designed by the Italians. The other was a collection of installations that, whether the museum understood it or not, deliberately set out to challenge, even to undermine the assumptions on which the rest of the exhibits were based.

So it was that at the museum's dinner to mark the opening on 23 May 1972 (just ten weeks after Sottsass's friend Feltrinelli had been found dead in a Milan suburb apparently trying to black out the city's electricity grid) two very different groups of Italian designers found themselves somewhat awkwardly in the same room. Whilst his cultural assumptions might have differed from the others, Sottsass was just as capable of creating a beautifully considered aesthetically resolved object as any of the characters on the other side of the ideological divide.

On one side of the trustees' dining room on the top floor of the museum's Edward Durrell Stone building were Sottsass and Andrea Branzi, on the other Mario Bellini and Gae Aulenti. The radicals versus those who were cast in the role of standing for conventional good taste. In the presence of the Rockefeller family, the Italians were on their best behaviour. Ambasz had organized the seating plan according to the familiarity of the visitors with English. Andrea Branzi captured the spirit of the event in an exuberant report in *Domus*. Sottsass arrived for the opening:

> ...on the bonnet of a taxi, driving the wrong way down the
> Avenue of the Americas, dressed in Mexican style and a
> pink tutu, and look, here are the Archizoom 13, with asbestos
> on the soles of their shoes, and open shirts to show off
> their transistor medallions, and La Pietra in an orange lamé
> suit with an electric tie.
> Here's Aulenti and Pesce, and Mickey Mouse, and
> Mendini from *Casabella*. And [even more fancifully] Dean
> Martin, Zsa Zsa Gabor and Frank Sinatra [...] at midnight
> the Madonna appeared on top of the Empire State,
> far to the south, and there was Emilio Ambasz in a tiny
> plane, skywriting 'Italy the New Domestic Landscape.'

In the exhibition itself, Sottsass's cabinets in moulded fibreglass bore a close resemblance to the components that he had shaped for the Elea computer fifteen years before. Bellini, however, had produced one of the more striking projects: a concept car, known as the Kar-a-sutra, which reconfigured the basic architecture of automobile design in a way that prefigured the people-carrier format eventually produced by Renault as the Espace and subsequently by many other manufacturers.

164

Sottsass's personal turmoil came to an end when his relationships with both Grau and his wife ended, and he started living with Barbara Radice, in the summer of 1976. In professional terms it was also the year when he began to take a renewed interest in the possibilities offered to a designer by a commercial brief. Together with Andrea Branzi he worked on the design of fashion designer Elio Fiorucci's New York shop. And even more provocatively, Branzi and Sottsass worked together on a customized special-edition Alfa Romeo Giulietta for Fiorucci, that had a thick pointillist skin, thick as porridge and flecked with colour; a design that looked a lot like a Memphis outlier. Sottsass had emerged from his crisis and was ready for something new.

Memphis

167

Among the 800 or so objects that Alessandro Mendini gathered together for his exhibition on the recent history of Italian design 'Quali cose siamo' ('The Things We Are') in March 2010, he found enough room for a kitsch reproduction of Michelangelo's David, a two-metre (six-foot) high Ferragamo shoe, a Mussolini-era steel helmet and an exquisite still life by Giorgio Morandi. But in all the main galleries of the Milan Triennale there was only one reference to Ettore Sottsass and it was an artefact that could be understood in a variety of ways, just as the ever-subtle Mendini intended. Hanging on the wall behind the plaster David, as white as a bucket of mozzarella, was a small oil painting of a full-length naked, as opposed to nude, Sottsass. It was painted by Roberto Sambonet, sometime in the second half of the 1980s, presumably from the life. Sambonet had an unsparing, unsentimental eye. The portrait is by no means a masterpiece, but it is unusual and striking in its frankness. It shows Sottsass as an isolated but solid figure, standing his ground, despite the vulnerability of his worn body and sagging belly, no longer the young athlete of the 1930s. His face is as lined as a ploughed field and his arms hang resignedly by his sides.

It was a curious way for Mendini to draw attention to the highly visible contribution that Sottsass had made to Italian design over the past half century. But perhaps that was not Mendini's purpose. A sharper reading of its inclusion would be to see the presence of the painting as a settling of scores between Mendini and Sottsass. It was intended, perhaps, to be understood as a reminder of Sambonet himself more than of the subject of his picture. Sambonet was a man who, after training as an architect, worked as a designer, producing elegant glass and metal domestic objects, as well as on such corporate identity programmes as a cloverleaf logo for the Lombardy region with Bob Noorda. Sambonet, who died in 1995, had become increasingly interested in painting later in his life.

'Quali cose siamo' was an elegantly displayed, sometimes baffling, sometimes infuriating, cabinet of curiosities; the summation of Mendini's life-long distrust of the materialism of design, and a reflection of both his charm and his perversity. It is unlikely that the Maoist student revolutionaries who stormed the Triennale in 1968 would have found it any more to their liking than Giancarlo de Carlo's exhibition. Other than the most fundamental one, '*Quali cose siamo*' made no explicit judgements about the objects that it was showing. It was an exhibition, ostensibly a design exhibition, staged in a museum of design, which appeared to have almost nothing in the way of self-conscious design in it. However, the message could not simply be taken as a celebration of design without designers. Ferragamo, a celebrity shoe designer, was not exactly anonymous. The exhibition was a celebration of the things that Mendini liked. It concentrated on the anonymous and the non-designed objects all around us that, as Mendini sees it, are more creative and more interesting than the self-conscious ones. However, Mendini is not interested in design without designers in the way that Bernard Rudofsky would have been. For Mendini anonymity comes with a stronger range of flavours than folk craft.

Of course it is not really the case that anything is entirely anonymous. A little more curatorial effort, and Mendini could have put a name and a date to the individual or individuals responsible for the steel helmet of the kind that Sottsass wore as an officer in the Alpini in Montenegro and on the Gothic line. Most of the supposedly anonymous works of design — the banal and the everyday that Mendini has been enthusiastic about ever since the 1970s — are the work of individuals, but the exhibition was notably short on information and explication. Mendini left his visitors to make their own conclusions.

He included only one Olivetti product from what can be called the conventional canon of modern Italian design, the Lettera 22 portable typewriter, designed not by Sottsass but by his predecessor Marcello Nizzoli. Was Mendini trying to suggest that Sottsass was not all that had been claimed during his lifetime? He never said so, but the choice of the Sambonet portrait could be understood as a reflection of the long, sometimes warm, sometimes fraught relationship between the two men.

There had been times when the two designers were closely aligned. Sottsass and Mendini first worked together in 1970, the year that Mendini became the editor of *Casabella*. When Sottsass went to Barcelona, Mendini sometimes went with him. Mendini was there at the dinner at MoMA in 1972 for the opening of 'Italy: The New Domestic Landscape'. When Mendini left *Casabella* and took over editorship of *Domus* in 1976, he made Sottsass the art director. 'I wanted the magazine to stand out on the shelves of the newsstands, so Sottsass had the idea of putting a black-and-white check pattern around the edge of the pages,' Mendini explained to me. But what might be seen as the greatest single triumph of Sottsass's career — the establishment of Memphis, a design movement that became instantly famous, discussed all over the world of design, was highly influential on the look of a generation of products, and in which Sottsass was the unchallenged leader of a substantial group of talented younger designers — was achieved at the expense of Mendini.

By the time that Memphis was being talked about, Sottsass had been living with Barbara Radice, who was to become his second wife, for almost four years. She was in her early thirties when they met; he was almost sixty. Radice had interviewed Sottsass and the magazine in which the profile appeared had used the word 'Memphis' in the headline long before the movement was born. Radice's passionate relationship with Sottsass formed the context for the rest of both his professional and personal life. He lived and worked not in his studio, but on their continual travels, in hotel rooms and aeroplanes, in the bubble which they would share for the rest of his life.

Radice brought her critical perspective to the shaping of the ideas that underpinned Memphis: she was its chronicler and an effective spokesperson. Not a designer herself, she was an ever-present part of the group's discussions. With Sottsass, she shaped *Terrazzo,* the magazine that came to encapsulate their shared view of visual culture. Together they made Memphis the design phenomenon of its time.

Mendini was the leading figure in Memphis's predecessor, Alchymia. And Alchymia was based on much of the same antipathy to conventional ideas of what design could be, and the search for a new aesthetic, that drove Memphis. However, Memphis was able to reach outside the world of design, and Alchymia never did.

It was Alchymia that had begun to talk first about radical redesign and a rediscovery of the banal, the ordinary and the everyday. In June 1978, when Alessandro Guerriero, the founder of Alchymia and a co-founder of the Domus Academy, organized an exhibition at the Palazzo dei Diamanti in Ferrara (where Alessandro Mendini showed the Poltrona di Proust, his pointillist-decorated armchair, for the first time), Sottsass was also included along with Andrea Branzi.

Fashion designer Elio Fiorucci described Alchymia and Memphis as having been born on the same wave, and inspired by the same things, but of the two Alchymia was by far the dreamier. Guerriero was unapologetic about that characteristic. While he was capable of making one of a thing, he once said, 'to be asked to make two would be a problem'. He added, '[art critic] Gillo Dorfles used to call us pitiful makers of kitsch, I was delighted, it meant that he had understood us.' Alchymia was an ill-defined coalition, established in 1975, that encompassed filmmakers and performance artists, as well as designers, and even an actor looking like an Italian version of Grace Jones (albeit as styled by a considerably more amateurish choreographer than Jean-Paul Goude). Guerriero depended on Mendini for his critical reputation and for his position as the editor of *Casabella,* as well as his connection with Sottsass. On the other hand, without previous experience of realizing any design beyond his early days in the architectural studio established by Marcello Nizzoli, Mendini needed a workshop that could make his designs. Alchymia offered him that.

Branzi and Michele De Lucchi joined Mendini and Sottsass, bringing together under a single umbrella both the Florentine and the Milanese wings of Italy's radical design movement. Mendini was ready to accommodate the ramshackle nature of Guerriero's activities, continually putting on exhibitions (frequently without the money to bring back the exhibits, which meant that they began to go missing). Within the coalition there were those — particularly Branzi, Sottsass and De Lucchi — who could be understood as possessing strong formal abilities and interests, and there were others who did not.

Alchymia achieved a brilliant coup in 1979 with the Bau.Haus project, a collection of furniture designs from Mendini, Branzi and others that attracted a great deal of attention as a sideshow at the Salone del Mobile, with its provocative rejection of the notion of conventional good design and good taste. It set out to undermine and even to mock received wisdom about design, in some cases by reworking existing iconic objects. However Alchymia could occasionally lapse into self-indulgent pretension, half Dada, half Futurist.

Sottsass lost patience with Guerriero's increasingly vague grasp on the practicalities of making, as well as his complete lack of interest in manufacturing, and decided to do things differently. One year he was a member of Alchymia, the next he was not. By December 1980 he was ready to launch the movement that would soon be called Memphis. He took Michele De Lucchi with him and, along with Aldo Cibic, George Sowden, Marco Zanini, Nathalie Du Pasquier, Matteo Thun and Martine Bedin, together they formed the core of the new group. Mendini contributed to the first Memphis collection in an only partly successful spirit of ecumenicalism, but Branzi was more closely involved.

On Mendini's side of the split, the argument was represented as being entirely materialistic. As Mendini put it to Alice Rawsthorn in an interview for *W* magazine:

He [Sottsass] always wanted to talk about money, and
Alchymia wasn't a place where you could do that. So he
left and started Memphis. Sottsass said, 'Are you coming
with me or not?' And I said, 'No, I'll stay with Alchymia.'
But I did design something for the first Memphis collection.
Up until then we'd been friends and spoken every day.
I always remained friends with Sottsass — I'm not capable
of making enemies — but he didn't remain friends with me.
Though we became friends again when Memphis ended.

Andrea Branzi managed to maintain connections with both sides of the divide. His work with Alchymia had included refined and subtle commentaries on some of the iconic Italian designs of the past. His pieces in the first Memphis collection were surprisingly rigorous and he was later to transfer the mood of these projects to work for the mainstream Italian manufacturer Cassina, which was still producing the chair that he had designed for them in his days as a member of Archizoom.

Mendini has suggested more recently that the argument was not so much between Sottsass and himself, as between Sottsass and Guerriero. 'Sottsass asked me to join him, but I chose to stay with Guerriero.' However, he still suggests that it basically came down to money.

Barbara Radice accounted for the split from Alchymia differently. She describes it as being about competence. 'In Sottsass's eyes the only way to make a real impact was to move beyond the scruffy and makeshift world of art installations and galleries, and to professionalize the project.' She described Alchymia as a promoter of 'radical and sometimes shoddy projects.' Sottsass felt that Alchymia was no longer working and, in Radice's words 'needed a manufacturer who could not only make experimental prototypes but also finished pieces as alternatives to standard products.' Radice wrote that Mendini's interests:

...lay mainly in producing exhibitions. He failed to see
that in 1980 if such cultural enterprises were to succeed
they could not remain isolated provincial exercises in the
avant-garde or counter-culture, refined as they might be.
They had to have wider, higher ambitions, they had to
throw off their artistic aura to compete directly with industry

in quality, quantity and image. Alchymia had neither concerned itself with nor succeeded in setting up even the shadow of a sales organization.

By this stage, Sottsass had emerged from the pessimism that shaped his creative work in the early 1970s, and had re-engaged with the idea that design could take a positive position. Mendini continued to maintain a critical, pessimistic attitude to design. As Radice recalls:

It was an attitude that had been typical of the radical category. His analysis of the banal, his idea that designers should redesign existing objects for at least ten years before doing anything else. He had no studio, and relied on Alchymia until it became a workshop and a partner of his ideas and projects, this Alchymia that Sottsass and De Lucchi hoped would be Memphis. Memphis was born from those determined to look for different directions.

According to Radice, 'the name Memphis appears for the first time in a notebook of Michele De Lucchi's, alongside the date 11 December 1980, and the address, via San Galdino' which, in those days, was Sottsass's apartment. There was the famous episode of side two of Bob Dylan's *Blonde on Blonde* album playing over and over: 'Stuck inside of Mobile, with the Memphis blues again.' The conversation continued over the following days at the Pizzeria Positano and Memphis was conceived. Renzo Brugola, who had produced Sottsass's furniture designs for Poltronova and for Mario Tchou's apartment back in 1962, was recruited to manufacture the key pieces. Mario and Brunella Godani, owners of the Arc 74 showroom in Corso Europa, offered space for the first exhibition of the new collection. Ernesto Gismondi, owner of the Artemide lighting company provided the capital and became a major shareholder. The plan was to do something that would have a real impact, something that would change the way that designers thought about things, but also to make a mark in the real world, to make real objects that real people would buy and use.

The group also looked beyond Milan for recruits to make contributions to the first collection. Michele De Lucchi wrote in *Domus* for its issue in 2001 that marked the twentieth anniversary of the first Memphis collection:

We spoke with Isozaki, Kuramata and Umeda in Tokyo, Graves in New York, Mariscal in Barcelona, Hollein in Vienna, and suddenly the whole world seemed to agree about the need to do Memphis. Actually there were an awful lot of people who did not agree with us at all. But all of us felt that we were the lucky owners of the truth and all the others were utterly hopeless. What a stroke of luck Memphis was for me. It taught me the value of provocation, the sense of always looking for something new and different, the importance of questioning everything, above all habits, and not only those of aesthetics and form; and the awareness that a revolution of sorts can be sparked even by designing plates, tables and chairs.

Memphis also worked with a number of manufacturers interested in promoting their products by being associated with the project and with Sottsass. Abet was already producing patterned laminates. By supporting Memphis, they hoped to make laminates look fashionable. Lorenz was a clock-maker and manufactured Memphis clocks. There was a glass manufacturer and a ceramics business, the electronics company, Brionvega that made a Memphis TV, and Rainbow, a fabric printer. All of them got involved and invested their promotional budgets for 1980 in the Memphis project, not because they were expecting mainstream commercial products to emerge, but because they wanted to be associated with what had every sign of being a sensational event.

In the months leading up to opening of the exhibition, not a word was uttered, but a mood of anticipation was slowly being built up. Memphis was already being called the New International Style, mostly by its members. A lot was being promised in the way of a break with the past. Sottsass helped with some feverish prose that sounded a lot like Dylan's lyrics, about nothing much in particular. The tangible results of the Memphis conversations were unveiled the following September, and took the form of a total of fifty-seven objects, most of them brightly coloured. There were four tables, two coffee tables, a trolley, a screen, two chairs, eleven lamps, three clocks, a television set, eleven ceramic objects, two beds, assorted wardrobes, bookcases, chests of drawers, a sofa, a desk, an armchair and a hat stand.

Technically, these were relatively conservative products. They were made using utterly traditional woodworking techniques. The revolution here was not in technology. The materials were also humble enough; timber finished in lacquer or laminate predominated. What was most shocking was the colour palette — brash combinations of sweet-toothed nursery colours, with blunt patterns applied on laminates — and the wilful way in which Memphis approached form. The language of Memphis designers rejected simplicity, logic and clarity, and was inspired by a compelling mix of playfulness and ritual.

Since the days of the Bauhaus, designers had clung, however tenuously, to a package of principles that defined good taste or good design (which for years had been seen as synonymous). Resolution, integration and coherence were valued, along with logic and sobriety. Sottsass turned all that upside down. His bookshelves looked deliberately irregular and incoherent, but not crude. His sideboard was an inconsistent and apparently arbitrary eruption. He used irreverent pinks, baby blues and patterned laminates — for years anathema to those who maintained a sense that design had values.

In the period leading up to the first Memphis collection, design had lost its way. Modernism no longer had the moral authority it had once had. In such circumstances, Sottsass seemed like a man who knew what he was doing, even if what he was doing did look rather odd, and he quickly attracted a following that took its direction from him.

Sottsass himself deliberately set out to put a bomb under what he called the 'uniform panorama of good taste,' which he saw being churned out by manufacturers pandering to the élitism of the affluent. 'For forty years I've been trying to get rid of culture and to produce design that is part of everyday life.'

Yet Sottsass always maintained two distinct strands to his work. Even as the radicalism of Memphis was being born, he was still running an industrially focused studio that was working on ultra-thin keyboards for Olivetti, which certainly qualified as good taste. And Sottsass's remarkable gift for colour and shape underpinned his work in the Memphis context, just as it did for all his other projects.

Though every piece was virtually handmade, Sottsass insisted that he had nothing in common with the craft movement. 'They can all be produced by machines. Plastic laminate is made by machines as are all the other elements. We are using standard furniture-industry technology, and we have nothing to do with the craft revival.'

Sottsass rejected the label of Postmodernism:

At a certain moment some critics need a formula to describe a set of changes. But this particular formula is very dangerous because it doesn't communicate reality. Young people have been discussing the limitations of functionalism since the war. Postmodernism is a very intellectual operation in the USA, and I don't agree with it. They simply quote elements of ancient art forms, and put them together in new ways — an intellectual game. Such games are fun in themselves, but nothing to do with design.

   I am trying to get my references from everyday life. I am more like a stupid peasant than I am an intellectual. I'm employing vaguely 1950s imagery, it's true, but the patterns are taken from what I call non-cultural iconography — from ordinary things. I'm looking for the things that are forgotten by everybody. I'm taking things from the suburbs, not even the people who use them know that they are doing so. American Pop art also refers to the popular landscape, but there's a self-consciousness there that results from a commercial awareness on the part of big companies such as Coca-Cola. It's all too organized. There are, however, areas that do not so vividly reflect commercial necessities, they are just there. It's these that I'm interested in.

But, even if Sottsass sometimes accepted the claim that he was resurrecting the 1950s, looking back at the first Memphis collection, it looks like a lot more than nostalgia; it offered something that was distinctively its own.

My work is taken as a criticism of society, but the way that you produce even the most commonplace machine has to have a ritualistic aspect, and that is what I am trying to address. Every product that you have to buy changes your life in some way. It's not simply a neutral consumer product you are buying, a machine or a piece of furniture should be a real companion, not be against you, not something that you end up hating.

176

The Bauhaus didn't talk only about functionalism,
it also talked about the relationship between design and
industry, functionalism was very rhetorical and very purist,
but that was because the Bauhaus people had to fight
against the academicians with slogans that belonged to
their times; things are different now.

As the Italian critic Stefano Casciani has pointed out, Memphis was a provocative mix of high culture and popular culture. It was a critique of Modernist archetypes, but it was also a celebration of anonymous and unself-conscious design. The names that the group gave the pieces produced for that first collection — Carlton, Plaza, Splendid and the rest— were, as Casciani has noted, names associated with both grand hotels and humble guesthouses around the world, implying a crossover between the ordinary and the exceptional. The same crossover informed Sottsass when he pointed the others in the direction of the reuse of everyday elements of suburban Milanese milk bars, the patterns of the industrial vernacular, in evoking but also transforming the energy and directness of popular culture, and using them not just to mock but also supplant the language of high design.

Certainly that was the impulse that connected the Milanese designers at the core of the movement, mostly Italians but with a few British and French members. Michael Graves and Hans Hollein, however, were doing something entirely different. Their work represented out-and-out Postmodernism. The Japanese contingent was different again; Kuramata was personally close to Sottsass, but retained a delicate refinement even when subverting terrazzo by introducing chunks of broken Coca-Cola bottles into the mix. But the international spread, and the combination of some very young designers with veterans, helped to give Memphis the character of much more than a single collection or exhibition. Memphis made it clear that it had the ambition of being a movement with longevity.

The Memphis explosion certainly had the effect of eclipsing Alchymia. Those members who remained with the group after Sottsass and De Lucchi's defection could be forgiven for feeling that their thunder had been comprehensively stolen, even though the name Studio Alchymia was printed alongside that of all the individual designers who took part in the first Memphis collection. Alchymia appeared on the back of an invitation card to the opening party, along with Lorenz, Abet and Brionvega (who had contributed a television in a green-and-yellow crocodile-skin case). On the front of the invitation was a lurid dinosaur — an image that seemed to use the same graphic language that Elio Fiorucci had commissioned for his retail business.

When suppliers looked to work with the group, Memphis was pragmatic about extending its range from objects that depended on basic timber and laminate into other materials. Up & Up from Massa contributed their granite-and-marble-working expertise for Aldo Cibic's Belvedere in 1982. Toso Vetri d'Arte from Murano allowed for some striking glass pieces in 1982 and 1983. There were rugs from Du Pasquier in 1983 made by Elio Palmisano. However it was clear that after the first three years, the movement was running out of energy.

By 1985, the Memphis catalogue — designed by Christoph Radl from Sottsass Associati with Aldo Ballo's photographs — looked business-like. The number of new products being launched had shrunk to just ten pieces of furniture from Sottsass, De Lucchi, Sowden, Branzi, Cibic, Zanini and Du Pasquier, plus some ceramics from the same inner core. There was no longer a need to make a big international statement. The catalogue listed distributors in fourteen countries, from Lebanon to South Africa, and a showroom in Milan at via Manzoni 46.

On another level, Memphis was never quite what Sottsass had hoped it would be. His view was that the 'designer in principle did not want to have anything to do with one-offs or limited editions, and even less to do with art objects. What they wanted was not to make collectors' items but furniture to be sold in stores, taken home and used every day.' Memphis never achieved that ambition. It was closer to what the Wiener Werkstätte had been in the years before World War I; making very small numbers of decorative objects for a very small number of enlightened and wealthy consumers. In Memphis's case, Karl Lagerfeld bought an example of almost every piece that Sottsass designed and used them to furnish his Monte Carlo apartment. Memphis entered the language of popular culture and advertising. It made the world beat a path to Sottsass's studio, the recently established Sottsass Associati whose early membership coincided with the younger Memphis team. Doug Tompkins, the American entrepreneur behind the Esprit fashion chain, was impressed enough to hire Sottsass to create a bold new look for his shops around the world.

Vienna had seen a split in the ranks of the avant-garde and so too did Milan. The tension between Sottsass and Mendini, replicated that of Adolf Loos and Josef Hoffmann. Given Loos's polemical skills, he might be said to be the Viennese version of Mendini, with the more designerly Sottsass playing the

Hoffmann role, but it is not an entirely appropriate analogy. Loos's interest in archetypes and fusing art, design and architecture parallel those of Sottsass more than they do Mendini's less convincing command of form, detail and colour.

There was continuing friction with Mendini, to the extent that Sottsass stepped back from designing for Alessi where Mendini was the art director, and instead began working on collections for Guzzini, Alessi's rival in the tableware market. Sottsass and Alessi had been very close to each other, but Mendini took a more and more central role in advising Alessi on its future direction and that left less room for Sottsass. If there is a comparison to be made between Sottsass and Mendini, it is that Sottsass's confidence in colour and ability to work with form was integrated with his intellectual approach to the use of design as a means of communication. Mendini, while certainly an intellectual and a highly original thinker, ultimately lacked the ability to turn these ideas into convincing physical form. In 1988 there was a fascinating rapprochement. A Milan gallery commissioned a table for which Sottsass designed one end and Mendini the other. Sottsass produced a table with a two-legged object that changed materials as it came close to the end of the cantilevered top that is propped up by Mendini's contribution, a little barrel vault.

For Sottsass, the Memphis movement was an explosive beginning to his later career. It made him an extraordinarily visible figure, establishing his significance for a new generation for whom mainframe computers were ancient history. Memphis coincided with architectural Postmodernism but Sottsass himself never considered himself a Postmodernist, and neither did such designers as Sottsass's friend from Tokyo, Shiro Kuramata.

In reality, Memphis was made up of three distinct groups. First, the inner core, who could be seen as Sottsass's colleagues or disciples. Then there were the internationally famous, primarily Hollein, Graves and Kuramata, who went on with what they were doing already, but added a Memphis label. Finally, there were the hopeful try-outs; some, such as Peter Shire from the US, moved towards art after Memphis, while others, such as Javier Mariscal in Barcelona or Terry Jones from *i-D* magazine in London, flourished on their own account.

The inner core was dominated by Sottsass's exploration of form, which provided a language that was followed with varying degrees of conviction by the rest. But there were other strong voices within this group. George Sowden had his own approach that was distinctively different from the way in which Sottsass worked. Nathalie Du Pasquier, a self-taught illustrator and pattern designer who has since become a painter, brought other sensibilities. Their work, individually and together, related to the ideas that interested Sottsass, but were more than a simple restatement of his aesthetic approach.

In September 1981, the Memphis pieces looked shockingly new and transgressive. But fundamentally, the best of them represent the kind of ideas that had shaped Sottsass's work for at least the previous thirty years. In its early years, the Memphis movement seemed like a threat to those designers who were interested in working on low-key, undemonstrative, rational directions. It was also seen as a rebuke to the then fashionable Philippe Starck. ('Are you with us, or with Starck?' Ron Arad remembers Radice asking him.) However, the energy was inevitably hard to maintain. Matteo Thun made an early departure from the group. Sottsass was unimpressed when he heard that after one session with a potential client (Anna Anselmi of Bieffeplast, the company making Joe Colombo's Boby Trolley), Thun stayed behind after he had left and brought out his own drawings. George Sowden and Michele De Lucchi never joined Sottsass Associati, but continued to work with Olivetti and on their own.

The strongest Memphis pieces come from the first collection of 1981. Casablanca in red, yellow and white laminate speckled with black tone is clearly a descendant of the totem furniture that Sottsass had created for Mario Tchou's apartment twenty years before. At first sight it looks like a random collage, but put together the shelves, chests of drawers and cabinets combine into a single object. Carlton has a similar approach, using more pure colour, and what can be interpreted as jamming a stick-like figure on top of bookshelves that already have some books on them. Antibes, from 1981 by Sowden, is altogether more delicate-looking, a glass-fronted cabinet raised up on spindly legs, with Du Pasquier's design printed on the laminate sides. Sowden's preferred palette of blue, yellow and red, immediately suggests, to British eyes at least, the children's books created by Enid Blyton. Later Kuramata's tambour-fronted units were turned into mainstream commercial products in Holland by Pastoe. De Lucchi used a lot of blue and yellow, in particular in his zoomorphic Kristall side table, which resembled a little four-legged creature, a dog, its head turned into a flat yellow disc, the body a laminated box.

By 1986, while the greatest hits from the first few Memphis collections were still commercially available as part of the back catalogue, the presentation at the time of the Salone del Mobile was a project described as 'Dodici Nuovi — Twelve New', curated by Barbara Radice. The budget had clearly been cut back severely. The pieces were made for the most part by designers who were close to, or actually working for, Sottsass, including James Irvine,

Nicholas Bewick and Massimo Iosa Ghini. The catalogue looked a lot less convinced about the commercial appeal of what it was offering. There were no distributors and, curiously, there are no names for the pieces either, giving the whole undertaking a faintly perfunctory air by comparison with the conviction of what had gone before.

And then it was all over.

'Every strong idea lasts a very short time,' Sottsass said later. 'Cubism lasted three years, then went into Surrealism, and then maybe a new kind of Cubism, but real classical Cubism did not last. Strong ideas are strong, but they cannot be developed, they are what they are. They come down like bolts of lightning, they are there, but finite.'

Sottsass had given up on the Memphis project by 1986, or perhaps even earlier. For him, it was only the first three collections that were really interesting. Sottsass, as Radice put it, voluntarily released the members but Memphis was not really his to close down. It was a commercial undertaking with a brand that he did not own:

> The man who gave us the money to make the first Memphis
> exhibition bought the name Memphis for one million lire,
> because we didn't care about the name and we didn't know
> the value of the name. Subsequently this man thought
> that he possessed the whole idea of Memphis, and asked
> us to make more furniture to increase his sales. But that's
> when we had to say no, because we never wanted to make
> anything that could be 'marketable'. We split up.

Sottsass
Associati

183

Marco Zanini lives in Rio now. He has a Brazilian wife, a young child and an apartment overlooking the Atlantic in a plaster-and-stone faced 1950s block with mahogany doors. The lift doors are topped by an elderly floor indicator with a moving brass pointer above it. Zanini's flat has one of Nathalie Du Pasquier's paintings on the wall of the living room. Zanini made a special frame for it. The place is furnished with a selection of pieces that he designed during the Memphis years. He bought the flat with the proceeds of selling a two-room apartment left to him by his family in Italy. He did it before Brazil turned into an economic hot spot. It would be unaffordable now.

Looking back, Zanini sees his career in Italy as framed by two bleak events. The first was the kidnap and murder of politician Aldo Moro in Rome. He had just started working for Sottsass when he heard the news on that day in 1978. Twenty years later came the exposure of the 'Tangentopoli' bribery scandals in Milan that destroyed the country's political class, taking many leading professionals with it.

The Moro murder turned out to be the terrible beginning of an escape from the 'anni di piombo', or 'years of lead', and the start of a long and optimistic decade for Italy. It really seemed possible that the Italian economy could outpace that of Britain. The country was known in those years for its gifted entrepreneurs, its world-leading research and its designers. It was the time when Benetton and Armani built high-tech factories that transformed both manufacturing and fashion, and the bright young economists, emerging from Bocconi University, built up Milan as a financial centre. It was the most fruitful period for Sottsass Associati — perhaps the first successful example of an Italian design consultancy that could cover the whole range of design disciplines. It was a consultancy that allowed Sottsass to produce some of the most creative work of his career and to shape the face of mainstream design.

The Italian bribery scandals of the 1990s demonstrated that the long years of criminal violence in the south had leeched into the north's culture of political influence peddling. The country's institutions had been hollowed out, except for a group of magistrates trying to cut out corruption. There was no benign outcome; the scandal led to the disaster of the Berlusconi years.

When the commission for Milan's new international airport at Malpensa came in, the largest project that Sottsass Associati ever built, Zanini was effectively running the studio. The airport was not the most successful example of the studio's work. What makes it stand out is the fact that there was almost nobody else but Sottsass left untainted by political connections and backhanders who was in a position to take it on at the end of the 1990s. G14, the design group closely associated with the Socialist Party's pork barrel, was removed from the project when it became clear that the European Union's anti-corruption rules tied to its subsidies for the new building had been ignored. Sottsass made a brave, but ultimately unsuccessful attempt to make a new kind of airport. His approach was rooted in his experience of landing in Munich's pristine steel-framed airport. He later told James Irvine that it made him feel like a germ in a yoghurt factory.

Malpensa is based on a conventional off-the-shelf airport planner's diagram. What is not so conventional, before it was enlarged to deal with the Milan Expo of 2015, is the green, burgundy and cream interior. There are columns topped by capitals and rusticated walls that hint at classical precedents. The terminal is Sottsass's most uncomfortable confrontation with a world for which he clearly had little sympathy. It was a brave but flawed attempt to make his approach work on the largest possible scale; to give an airport some of the intimacy of a Sottsass domestic interior.

For Zanini, the scandals made Italy a diminished place in which it was increasingly difficult to work. He gave up his partnership in Sottsass Associati in 2002 and moved to Panama, where he spent a couple of years working on the Liquid Jungle Lab for Jean Pigozzi, part eco-research lab, part private island (a project that Sottsass himself was not interested in taking on). From there Zanini moved to Brazil and his apartment on the beach.

Zanini first met Sottsass in 1974. He was an architecture student at the University of Florence — in those days the intake was 2,500 students a year. It was chaotic but, thanks to the American exchange students, Florence had a much more international outlook than most Italian cities in the 1970s. Zanini was a student of Giovanni Klaus Koenig and Gianni Pettena. Koenig was a capable industrial designer, as well as an architect, whilst Pettena was more interested in the counter-culture.

Zanini, like Sottsass, was from the Trentino. He went to Florence for the sunshine, as he put it, but found a city at the centre of what seemed to be the most interesting thing on Italy's design landscape at the time: radical design. It was where Archizoom had been established by Andrea Branzi and Massimo Morozzi. It was Superstudio's base.

Quite what constituted radical design in the context of Italy is hard to define. It was more of an attitude than a coherent movement, one that owed a lot to the ideas that the Italians learned from international magazines such as *Architectural Design* that were full of the work of *Archigram*. The dome-builders and ecologists of California were an element in the mix. The *Whole Earth Catalog* excited Italian radicals, as did the squatters of London and Berlin. But there were also some echoes of the wilder dreams of the Futurists in the speculations of the Florentine architectural studios of the 1970s. Sottsass went to London and was enchanted by the King's Road, by Pop Art, by the underground press (*OZ* and *It* magazine in particular), by the mirrors of the Chelsea Drug Store, and the front half of a Cadillac protruding from the facade of Granny Takes a Trip at the lower end of the King's Road.

Pettena had a lot to do with setting up the Global Tools network. Alessandro Mendini put its thirty members, who included Andrea Branzi and Sottsass, on the cover of *Casabella*. Zanini made a reinforced concrete boat for Pettena. At the end of 1974 he drove his tutor's Renault 4 to London, and spent a month hanging around the Architectural Association.

Zanini met Sottsass in Milan. He went to a Global Tools event at an art gallery on the via Brera hoping to see him. Sottsass wasn't there, but the gallery gave him the address of Sottsass's studio, close by in the via Manzoni.

They talked for hours. As they were finishing, Sottsass asked Zanini where he was from, and the connection was made. Their families shared the same background of life in the mountain communities. It took three years for them to work together, but it was a meeting that changed both their lives. For Zanini, an ambitious provincial just setting out, it was a kick-start for his career. For Sottsass looking to find a way to face up to the challenges of a future without Olivetti, Zanini offered an injection of youthful energy without the friction of an intellectual challenge.

This was a difficult time for Sottsass. Constantly travelling to and from Barcelona every weekend to see Eulàlia Grau and shuttling Pivano to Rome to keep her out of the way was draining him of cash. And the situation was about to get still more complicated when Sottsass met Barbara Radice and left Pivano. He had to support his ex-wife, start a new home and find a new studio. Olivetti, his only regular source of income, was in decline. He needed money

186

badly and was trying to boost his work outside Olivetti. There was a failed attempt to set up a new studio called CDM with Branzi and others.

Zanini was still very young. After finishing his degree, and spending some time working in California, he accepted Sottsass's offer to work for him. In 1977, Zanini arrived at what was still Sottsass's Olivetti-financed studio on via Manzoni, where he worked alongside George Sowden. He brought with him Matteo Thun and Aldo Cibic whom he had met as students in Florence. Zanini's first project with the studio was a light for the German manufacturer Erco. Then there were collaborations on a champagne bucket for Alessi, the famous Fiorucci car that Sottsass did with Branzi, and a project for a museum in Berlin.

At the time, the two people that most design students in Italy wanted to work for were Marco Zanuso and Vittorio Gregotti, but where others saw a man reaching the closing days of his career, Zanini understood that there was something special about Sottsass. Their relationship became increasingly close. When Sottsass finally divorced Pivano, it was Zanini that he asked to organize moving her into a new home. The apartment above the studio in via Manzoni was sold, and a distraught Pivano was moved to a much smaller flat in the via Senato. She took a *Marilyn* print, a gift to the two of them from Andy Warhol, with her. Zanini also supervised the donation of thousands of Sottsass's drawings to the University of Parma's archive and when Sottsass's mother died — she had spent her last years in a retirement home in Trento next door to Zanini's old school — Sottsass asked him to organize the funeral.

Zanini's arrival coincided with the beginning of Sottsass's relationship with Radice. Zanini remembers going to Venice in 1976 to meet Sottsass and going to a retrospective exhibition of his work at the Museo Correr. There was a dinner at which he saw Pivano and Umberto Eco. Grau was still a distant presence. But while organizing that exhibition, Sottsass had met Radice.

Zanini remembers the financial strain that Sottsass was under:

> He was short of money all the time. I saw him asking Alba Monti, the office secretary, for cash for lunch. She would open the drawer and bring out some banknotes. It was the Continental that he would go to for lunch in the old days, then when it closed he shifted to the Torre di Pisa.
>
> On Fridays, to get through the weekend, he would say 'Alba, I need money.' And she would open the drawer and give it to him. Some days, he would say 'Is there no

more?' And she would say, "No, *architetto*, there is no more.' While I was there, a job came in to design a mobile home for Fiat. Nicola Tufarelli, who had been an Olivetti executive and then moved to become a manager at Fiat, was a very decent man. He knew that Ettore needed work and he gave him the job. The design needed to be ready for the Turin motor show in September 1978.

After the presentation, Sottsass and Zanini spent three weeks together over Christmas travelling around southern India. 'We flew back via Karachi and Tehran, where we were stuck on the tarmac for hours, it was the day that Khomeini came back from [exile in] Paris.'

It was during those weeks that Zanini talked to Sottsass about the future of the studio. He suggested the establishment of Sottsass Associati, with Matteo Thun and Aldo Cibic as their first partners. It was formally constituted in 1980. Sottsass Associati grew to employ fifty people. Memphis attracted clients from all around the world in a way that had never happened to Sottsass before. Among the new clients was Doug Tompkins, the fashion retailer from San Francisco who had started the North Face, a shop in North Beach that sold sports clothes, and who could remember Allen Ginsberg wandering in from the City Lights bookshop across the street, attracted by the photographs of muscled athletes. Tompkins wanted a new look for his worldwide chain of Esprit stores. Sottsass did a lot of them in Germany and Australia, and he also encouraged Tompkins to work with others. He introduced him to Shiro Kuramata and to Antonio Citterio.

Then there was Jean 'Johnny' Pigozzi, the mercurial heir to a French car factory fortune. Pigozzi became a close friend, staging glittering birthday parties for Sottsass each year in Antibes, commissioning him to design his apartments in London and New York, and to design the interiors of his yacht. Pigozzi, with the help of IDEO founder David Kelley, also commissioned Sottsass to work on the Enorme project. Enorme was meant to deliver a stream of stylish telecommunications devices, but was abandoned after the first of them (a telephone handset that was so expensive to make that it retailed for US$90, but had fewer features than its competitors, which could sell for a fraction of that price). Pigozzi introduced Sottsass to Helmut Newton. Another client was gallerist Bruno Bischofberger, who was not only Sottsass's dealer but also commissioned him to build a house in Switzerland.

To cope with its growing numbers of employees, the firm moved from via Manzoni, first to the basement in the via Borgonuovo that Sottsass had been using as his private studio, then to via Melone. Sottsass's Olivetti studio moved into the Corso Venezia alongside that of Mario Bellini.

Sottsass Associati was unusual in the Italian context, where most design studios are based on a single individual and, in general, focus on a single discipline. Sottsass recruited a range of partners with different interests. Thun, Cibic and Zanini had all trained as architects. Christoph Radl, an Austrian born, like Sottsass, in Innsbruck, who joined the firm in late 1980, was different. He had studied graphic design in Milan. He worked with Sottsass on print for Memphis and developed the packaging and brand identity for Alessi and later for Ansaldo. Radl ended up art directing *Terrazzo*, the last, most elaborate and best-funded of the magazines that measured out Sottsass's career. Radl's graphic work took him from branding to advertising, not a subject that Sottsass at this stage was interested in. Radl set up a small advertising agency, alongside his partnership in Sottsass Associati, which for a while retained a stake in the consultancy. Marco Susani had been more involved with electronics and, after the Enorme project ended, Susani became head of design at Motorola.

Sottsass Associati had a worldwide reach and worked on furniture, graphic design, electronics, products, interiors and, increasingly, on architecture. There was a fluctuating cast of partners who came and went, resulting in the wide range of its work, and some sometimes strikingly different vocabularies. Sottsass himself always had the ability to work simultaneously on glass and jewellery pieces and limited editions that had a very different approach from the industrial work. Also unusual in the Italian context was the number of non-Italian partners. James Irvine, Gerry Taylor and Chris Redfern were from Britain. Johanna Grawunder came from the USA.

After Zanini left, the character of the firm changed. Ernest Mourmans, the Dutch gallerist who worked closely with Sottsass on making a series of increasingly elaborate limited editions in glass and ceramics, marble and rare woods, became a partner and a close friend. As Sottsass entered his late eighties and became less mobile, Mourmans was a solicitous and protective presence. Chris Redfern, who was just twenty-four when he arrived, became a partner at twenty-six, and maintained the industrial side of the much-reduced scale of the practice. At the time of Sottsass's death, there were just three partners: Sottsass himself, Mourmans and Redfern.

Sottsass was never ready to limit himself to working within the boundaries of his own studio. What he always looked for was the stimulus of other people. Irvine, who came to Milan to work for Olivetti, and then ended up in Sottsass's studio remembers how Sottsass always tried to engage with others:

> Ettore was called by Rolf Fehlbaum of Vitra. 'I want
> you to work on an experiment about the future of the
> office.' Sottsass was interested but said, 'That is too
> big for me alone. Let's work with Branzi and De Lucchi.'
> I was the coordinator on the Citizen Office project.
> Ettore did an office chair with a rucksack on the
> back and a meeting room as a tent. Branzi did a vertical
> office. Branzi's ideas had an artistic value rather than
> offering a strategy for design, but Ettore always stayed
> in touch with human needs.

Irvine remembered both the benefits and the challenges of working for Sottsass, a creative force of nature that could be difficult to share a room with. For Irvine, maintaining a certain independence in the studio was vital. 'He would guide you with a quick sketch, but what was so important was to avoid turning into a horrible fake Ettore. What you had to learn from Ettore was not his style, but his ability to take something entirely ordinary, like a spoon for Alessi, and to turn it into something special.'

What Sottsass looked for in his associates was the ability to handle those aspects of a project that no longer engaged him. The British and American designers in the studio brought with them the kind of practical competence that Italian universities did not teach. Apart from Radl, most of them were industrial designers, but there was one young woman, Johanna Grawunder, who had an architectural background, and who was to be essential in the last phase of Sottsass's career as an architect. Sottsass always saw himself as an architect, and was frustrated not to have his architectural work achieve the recognition that he believed it was due. It was only after the success of the Memphis movement that he was able to secure the kind of commissions that gave him the chance to put his ideas to work.

Sottsass did not care for overbearing or monumental architecture and he was reluctant to identify with the Postmodernism that had taken hold of architecture in the 1980s. He was interested in archetypes, shrines, doorways, thresholds and tombs. And in this it is possible to see the origins of his sympathy for Aldo Rossi, an architect who also had a facility for drawing and a preoccupation with images that could embody collective memories of the idealized forms and elements of a traditional city.

The architectural projects that Sottsass designed and built in the 1980s and 1990s were, for the most part, private houses, the kind of project that depends on an intense involvement and building personal relationships with a client. There were others, of which Malpensa is the largest and the most impersonal. There was also an exotic golf resort built in China for a company owned by the army. The houses were of a scale that could also be comfortably designed by Sottsass working almost on his own, with just one key assistant.

Johanna Grawunder studied architecture at California State Polytechnic, but spent the final year of her course in Florence. She stayed on to work in Italy rather than going home to America. Sottsass Associati offered her a job in 1985, just as Sottsass was beginning to get significant architectural commissions. She became a partner in 1989 as Sottsass began to depend on her for making the architectural projects happen. They built a series of houses around the world together. The first of these, completed in 1989, was in Colorado for Daniel Wolf, a businessman married to Maya Lin, who as a young architecture student had won a competition to design the Vietnam War Memorial in Washington.

Wolf was an enthusiast and he asked Sottsass simply to do the house that he had always dreamed of building. According to Grawunder, Wolf actually suggested that he wanted Sottsass 'to build his Falling Water'. The house was substantial, on a remote rural site, and was in some ways the realization of the sketches that had filled Sottsass's notebooks over the years, full of exotic marble and lush timbers. The last and perhaps the most lavish in the sequence was a house for Ernest Mourmans in Belgium.

Grawunder remembers that Mourmans had first come to Sottsass in the hope of becoming his gallerist. 'Ettore said, "no, I am already represented by Bruno Bischofberger, so I can't do a show with you. But we can do an exhibition of designs made by Johanna working with me."' It was a means for Sottsass to get the measure of Mourmans, a wealthy young Dutch architect and collector-turned-dealer, who was to shape the last act of Sottsass's career.

Mourmans worked with a series of designers including Gaetano Pesce, Ron Arad and Sottsass, and then subsequently with the artist John Chamberlain. Mourmans is a tall, imposing, bulky figure with a ponytail, a taste for black Bentleys and leather coats, and a manic work rate. Unlike most people in his position,

Mourmans is fascinated by making, fabricating and using his own hands as well as assembling teams of expert craftsmen and sourcing exotic and precious materials.

The house that Sottsass, working with Grawunder, designed for him is on the Belgian side of the border near Maastricht, and it is perhaps the most flamboyant of all Sottsass's domestic projects. Apart from design, Mourmans has two other passions. One is for endangered bird species, Sottsass's starting point for the project, the other is for exotic cars.

Half house, half aviary, it has been designed for its bird and human occupants to interact to an unusual extent, while the cars are hidden away in an underground garage. A treble-height aviary slices right through the collection of pavilions rising out of a lake that constitute the house. Two of the pavilions are devoted to birdlife, the rest are for people. Each of the children get their own house within the house — which is to say that each of them has a self-contained suite of rooms with their own internal staircase.

The setting is suburban, at one end of a street lined by substantial recently built houses on the edge of a wooded landscape, and offers little in the way of a starting point for the design of the house. Sottsass chose to fragment the house into a series of interconnected elements. It is a strategy that protects the privacy of the house and at the same time serves to create its own landscape. From every window, what you see most of is the architecture of the house itself. The largest two volumes are the kitchen, on the street side of the house, and the living room, a double-height space with a mezzanine for the library. This space, with an external colonnade and terrace jutting out into the lake is the pivot around which the design is based. The arrangement is neither formal nor picturesque. Sottsass enjoyed surrealistic jumps of scale, and took pleasure in the physicality of architecture. Sottsass and Grawunder designed all the furniture — except the chairs in the kitchen which are replicas of those found at Harry's Bar in Venice. The fireplaces and the bathrooms are theirs too, alongside a number of set pieces, a swimming pool decorated with a Helmut Newton mural, a bed with drapes designed by Issey Miyake, a Dan Flavin light piece in the entrance hall and a wall-painting by Francesco Clemente.

Grawunder began working on the 'Birdhouse', as the project became known, in March 1996 and it took another seven years to complete. At the time Grawunder and Sottsass were working simultaneously on two more houses in Belgium for members of the Mourmans family, on the house for Bischofberger in Switzerland, on another house on Maui and on a group of houses in Singapore. A little later David Kelley acquired a site in Palo Alto. Each house has its own inflections. In Switzerland planning restrictions dictated the form of the house. And the interior needed to have qualities to show off Bischofberger's fluctuating collection of twentieth-century masterworks. Sottsass eventually suggested black stone walls as the best option. Kelley was content to allow Sottsass to take the lead on most aspects, but insisted on having space indoors for his Harley Davidson.

Mourmans' house took the longest to complete, as the client followed his passion for sourcing every detail himself, finding rare timbers and exotic masonry. Grawunder and Sottsass went to see the site while building Mourmans' sister's house nearby. As they walked towards it, they found the structure that Mourmans had built for his birds. Mourmans talked about the number of bedrooms he would need. He wanted a large open kitchen that would merge into a living area. He asked for a large master bedroom and bathroom, the multi-car garage and an indoor pool. The aviary, however, did not come up.

Sottsass responded with a series of sketches for the Birdhouse, which showed the aviary as an integral part of the building, and which made all the children's rooms separate volumes. 'Little private houses with lofts,' as Grawunder puts it. She took Sottsass's sketches and turned them into a 1:200 scale plan, regularizing the geometry, adding in the technical details that would make the circulation, the garage and pool areas work. Then she made a painted Styrofoam model to show Sottsass. The details evolved but the form and plan are essentially what she had shown him in that model.

Mourmans knew a Dutch ceramic tile manufacturer that could turn Helmut Newton's photograph into a wall mural for the pool. Sottsass and Newton chose the specific image. Grawunder kept postponing designing the light fitting that Sottsass and Mourmans asked her to make in the corner of the staircase, until Sottsass advised Mourmans to install the Dan Flavin there instead.

Sottsass had designed a canopy bed for the 'Fase Alternativa' ('Alternative Stage') exhibition at Abitare il Tempo in Verona in 1997. Mourmans had the bed made and after the show it was set aside for the house. The corridor leading from the entry to the living room on the ground floor was designed specifically for a collection of Sottsass ceramics that Mourmans had commissioned.

The centrepiece of the kitchen is a large table. Sottsass made it a little lower than normal, to allow it to be used with lounge chairs that could encourage people to spend an entire evening there rather than retreating into a living room after dinner. For it to work the idea needed the right kind of chair. Sottsass and Grawunder were talking about the project in Harry's Bar, and decided that the armchairs they were sitting in would do the job very well. They were introduced to the factory that made them for the Ciprianis and ordered a special batch.

Mourmans and Sottsass pursued a shared interest in making use of special materials and techniques. It meant that there was no conventional builder and no supervising architect. Grawunder remembers:

> For the interior finishes, we designed each room and drew every single wall and detail. We positioned the doors and frames, showed how the baseboards lined up with this or that, the switches and all cabinets and fixtures, and Ernest then made sure these details were executed perfectly.
>
> Mourmans ran the contract himself. His input was fundamental. Initially, his main input, beyond the programme, was setting the scale and ambition of the architecture; pushing and encouraging Ettore to go beyond what we had built before. Then, with the interiors and finish materials, his involvement was even more direct and decisive as he steered the interiors to the richness that makes the house and surfaces so stunning. The Brazilian blue stone floor and the exotic timbers were extremely rare and hard to find. My puritan side started feeling a bit uneasy at a certain point, I think it was when I learned the price of the Brazilian blue. But Ettore embraced it and was grateful for this kind of intensity. His Austrian side no doubt.
>
> Ernest and Ettore seemed to understand each other immediately. Even when Ettore was still testing the waters with the design collections he did together with Ernest, there always seemed to be a very similar understanding and respect for certain things, be it marble, fancy woods, lacquers, food, sex. Ernest's knowledge and expertise about all kinds of things (from birds to flowers to steel) seemed to hit a nerve with Ettore.
>
> At a certain point in the construction, when most of the structure and exterior finishes were in, I went less and less to the site and Ettore went often without me. This was

very unusual and in fact, there is no other project we did together where Ettore basically took over my job. Usually at a certain point I did the day-to-day troubleshooting. But with Ernest, he did not need the sort of translator/defender of the architecture figure I would normally have to become during construction of a project.

Grawunder sees Sottsass's architectural work as a sequence, bookended by the two most vivid houses. Casa Wolf starts the sequence explosively, full of the richness and flamboyance that Sottsass had waited so many years to realize in the four decades since he had effectively given up the practice of architecture. The Birdhouse is as ambitious, grand and sculptural, and has lost the hints of Postmodernism that can be found in Casa Wolf. The houses between these two bookends are what Grawunder calls:

> ...more reasonable, not lesser, but somehow more achievable. I always think of David Kelley's house in California as the calm, morning-after project from the drunken, wild-binge project of the Birdhouse. The plan and volumes are very similar in their 'percorso' (first-person shooter) way of navigating the architecture, but they are delineated and scaled much more modestly than the Birdhouse.

Grawunder left the partnership in 2001 to concentrate on her own design work rather than architecture. And in his last years, Sottsass focused on the series of edition pieces that he made with Mourmans. Sottsass was a man who had come close to death more than once in the course of a long life. Like Picasso, he drew on the energy of sexuality to maintain his sense of creative purpose but, unlike Picasso, he remained consistent in the language that he used for his work. He had clarity, and the ability to use drawing to convey the essence of an idea, and to a remarkable extent, through his ability to spot talent, maintained that clarity in the output of Sottsass Associati.

Epilogue

197

For Sottsass the end of a year was always an important day. He marked most of them with a drawing or a card that he sent to his friends. In 1944, there could be nothing more than a letter to his parents written in the semi-darkness of an abandoned railway tunnel in Tuscany, barricaded against the advancing Americans. In 1968 it was a particularly elaborate production: a long folded strip of paper, illustrated with a mix of Sottsass's drawings and found images of a variety of deities and shrines. The first sheet has Sottsass's drawing of a pair of hands raised in namaste. The handwritten note reads: 'Fernanda Pivano and Ettore Sottsass, resident at 14 via Manzoni, Milan 20121, call upon Shiva and Mohammed, Christ and Krishna, and Itzamna and the Mother Goddess, Buddha and all the gods of Egypt, Zeus, the constellations and above all Ishtar, to protect you for the whole of 1968.'

In 1999, he produced a booklet, with no words, just the numbers from 1 to 365. At the end of 2005 it was a tarot card with the names of the remaining Sottsass Associati printed on the back to offer best wishes for 2006. The following year, he produced a sheet of paper, folded three times. The larger section had a black ink drawing by Sottsass, a seemingly incomprehensible scribble. Beneath, printed in red in Sottsass's always clear, urgent capital letters.

> It seems to me that the world today is in a dangerous state of deadly widespread confusion. Am I right? Let's all hope the confusion will end next year, or at the least, keep away from us, and not affect us.

It is signed Ettore and Barbara, and dated the first of January 2007.

Ettore Sottsass died on the last day of 2007.

Author's acknowledgements

This book has been shaped by conversations with many people, a number of whom are no longer alive, notably Ettore Sottsass himself. I met him in 1981 in the aftermath of the party that launched the first Memphis collective exhibition. I saw him again increasingly often, especially in the four years I spent in Milan as the editor of *Domus*. There were occasional lunches at the restaurant Torre di Pisa, a weekend at the house he built for Ernest Mourmans, a trip to see the house that he made for Bruno Bischofberger, and visits to exhibitions of his work at the Glasgow School of Art and at the Design Museum in London.

I also had the chance to meet two key figures in Sottsass's development before they died: Aldo Rossi and Shiro Kuramata. James Irvine, who died sadly young in 2013, played an essential part in this book both for his own remarkably sharp view of what it meant to be a designer working in the orbit of Sottsass's genius and for his help in navigating the world of design in Italy. Johanna Grawunder, who is flourishing in California, patiently took me through Sottsass's working methods as an architect. Both Johanna and James were generous interpreters diverting attention from my rudimentary Italian in conversations with Andrea Branzi, and Enzo Mari.

George Sowden, Nathalie Du Pasquier, Gerry Taylor, Marco Zanini, Perry King, Emilio Ambasz, Rolf Fehlbaum, Jean Pigozzi, Fernando Amat, Doug Tompkins and Alessandro Mendini, were also generous with their time. I thank them all for their insights and advice. Any shortcomings in this book are my responsibility and not theirs. I am also particularly grateful to Joe Pickard and Emilia Terragni at Phaidon.

Bibliography

Bozzer, Alessio and Mascellani, Beatrice, Eds., *Ettore Sottsass. Vorrei Sapere Perche / I Wonder Why*, exhibition catalogue (Milan: Electa, 2007)

Carboni, Milco and Radice, Barbara, eds., *Ettore Sottsass: Scritti 1946-2001* (Vicenza: Neri Pozza Editore, 2002)

Fernanda Pivano. Viaggi Cose Persone, exhibition catalogue (Milan: Silvana Editorial, 2011)

Fiaschi, Cesare, *La Guerra sulla Linea Gotica Occidentale. Divisione Monterosa 1944-45* (Bologna: Lo Scarabeo, 1999)

King, Perry, Shapira, Nathan H. and Von Klier, Hans, Eds., *Design Process Olivetti 1908-1978* (Milan: Olivetti, 1979)

Kircherer, Sybille, *Olivetti (Design Management)* (London: Trefoil Publications Ltd, 1988)

Maffei, Giorgio and Tonini, Bruno, eds., *Books by Ettore Sottsass* (Mantua: Corraini Edizioni, 2010)

Morrison, Kenneth, *Montenegro: A Modern History* (London: I.B. Tauris, 2009)

Ochetto, Valerio, *Adriano Olivetti. La Biografia* (Roma: Edizioni di Comunità, 2013)

Pivano, Fernanda, *Diari (1917-1973)* (Milan: Bompiani, 2008)

Radice, Barbara, *Memphis: Research, Experiences, Results, Failures and Successes of New Design* (London: Thames and Hudson, 1985)

Redžić, Enver, *Bosnia and Herzegovina in the Second World War* (London: Routledge, 1998)

Sottsass, Ettore, *Scritto di Notte* (Milan: Adelphi Edizioni, 2010)

Sottsass, Ettore, *The Curious Mr Sottsass: Photographing Design and Desire* (London: Thames and Hudson, 1996)

Sparke, Penny, *Ettore Sottsass, Jnr.* (London: The Design Council, 1982)

Index

Phaidon Press Limited
Regent's Wharf
All Saints Street
London N1 9PA

Phaidon Press Inc.
65 Bleecker Street
New York, NY 10012

www.phaidon.com

First published in 2015
© 2015 Phaidon Press Limited

ISBN 978 0 7148 6953 7

A CIP catalogue record for this book
is available from the British Library.

Commissioning Editor: Emilia Terragni
Project Editor: Joe Pickard
Production Controller: Steve Bryant
Design: James Goggin, Practise
Printed in China

Picture credits:

Images 1-5: photographer unknown
Images 6-7: courtesy Perry King
Image 8: courtesy Johanna Grawunder
Image 9: courtesy Philip Sayer